ArtUReady?

"It is not good for man to be alone"

~

"A woman's desire is for her man" (Genesis 3:16)

Ola Gilkey

© 2017 ArtConfetti

These are writings and references of hope, faith, motivation and enlightenment based on and influenced by the inspired Word and stories from the Bible. As applicable, the fiction events and characters described herein are imaginary and are not intended to refer to specific places or living persons. No part of this ArtUReady? book may be reproduced transmitted or stored in whole or part in any form or by any electronic, graphic or mechanical means including information storage and retrieval systems without express written permission from the publisher, except in the case of brief quotations embodied in critical articles and reviews. All rights reserved. Except as otherwise noted, all works of art are ®© by Ola Gilkey © ArtConfetti. Published by: Ola Gilkey (for ArtConfetti) Cover design and illustrations: By Ola Gilkey Artconfetti.com logos are trademarks belonging to Ola Gilkey.

ArtConfetti ISBN:9780984647415

Copyright © 2017 Ola Gilkey

All rights reserved. ArtUReady?

Table of Contents

Dedication	Page 4
Foreword	Page 6
Introduction	Page 10

Chapters

1	Chapter What is your dress size?	Page 21
2	Chapter What color should I wear?	Page 27
3	Chapter Be a Fruit Inspector	Page 35
4	Chapter Set the Guy Free	Page 38
5	Chapter Is the Doctor In?	Page 40
6	Chapter Put Money on It	Page 47
7	Chapter Out of Order	Page 52
8	Chapter TTYL	Page 61
9	Chapter The Flying Nelson	Page 66
10	Chapter "Phonie Bolognie"	Page 72
11	Chapter The Next Big Deal	Page 75
12	Chapter Phlatt Stanlie	Page 78
13	Chapter Meatloaf	Page 83
14	Chapter Can't You Feel That?	Page 90
15	Chapter Good Knight	Page 94
16	Chapter Concentration	Page 96
17	Chapter "The Life of Riley"	Page 98
18	Chapter Wing Gate	Page 102
19	From the Author	Page 109
Minuet		Page 111

Poems

My Happy	Page 19
Paint	Page 33
Set the Guy Free	Page 38
Phlatt Stanlie	Page 81
Scars	Page 92
Perhaps	Page 107

DEDICATION

This book is dedicated to my parents, Henry and Iola Gilkey. To my beautiful daughter: You are every beat of my heart and I pray God's covering and protection on your daily life. I love you!!! This book is also dedicated to the three most charming children in my life, my grandchildren. They are the inspiration for my journey through this book. I pray for them God's love, peace and protected elevation as they grow closer to Christ. I pray that they receive Jesus Christ as their Lord and Savior and that they fulfill the assignment for their lives with truth and grace. I pray their unique gifts and talents will be a blessing to others and the pleasure of their existence. As grandchildren go, they are the best! I also pray that the Lord will bless and keep all the children, family and friends. Remember my children, stay strong, be of good courage and work hard: David & Goliath: David was a youth when he defeated Goliath. He was obedient and diligent (I Samuel 17: 12-32). He trained (I Samuel 17:32-37), he was confident (I Samuel 17: 48-53). You can do it (Hebrews 10: 35-36)! I love you, Nana.

Acknowledgments

Who dat? Thank you to all!

Foreword

ArtUReady? is a book written to help us examine some of the glaring and less noticed subtle areas of relationships and how we through self-exploration and reflection, can personally and Spiritually mature (through negative and positive experiences). We are generally aware and reminded of the major aspects and pitfalls of relationships that set traps for failure. Like the serial dysfunctional daters; compulsive liars, the multiple "baby mama" guy, the guy who lacks ambition, the guy who dates two sisters, the mother and the daughter dater, the physical abuser, etc. These guys (and gals) types represent "red flags" for all who are seeking a wholesome relationship. When other people, tell you to take a "detour" of these menaces if their journey crosses your path (because they know their reputation); then you are foolish not to heed the warning. So, if you are young, we offer this sage, early advice; have only one romantic relationship; to evade this kind of unnecessary pain and damage of your life.

These people should be avoided because of their corruptible influence on any well intended relationship. There is major post traumatic syndrome (PTS) work and repair for these emotionally disturbed individuals, so let their reckless behavior miss you until they get help. Their heart needs repair and return to selflessness, sharing, sympathy, empathy and sensitivity. Prayer and Spiritual introduction and/or renewal are what they need most to get healing (not use you as a target to unleash bad behavior). Older folks have been casualties or perpetrators of this behavior. These big issues hopefully are easy "no brainers" to dodge and avoid. However, as well, there are those little things that creep in to undermine two terrific people from truly enjoying harmony and matrimony. For example, either we don't know, or we realize too late that past hurts or unresolved pain has robbed us of a wonderful relationship. Exploring information about what could "really be going on" can help us understand and remedy problems between two wonderful people that God has brought together.

In addition, we don't highlight the positives (encouragement, celebrating one another, thankfulness, etc.); those niceties that we sometime over look, that endear couples and cement their relationship, are important and need to be in the forefront.

This book intends to explore some considerations to bridge both sides. "The obvious writing on the wall" is also information that can help us determine if a person in the relationship is not sent by God and if we should turn our focus and attention quickly away to a more fruitful relationship. To enjoy true companionship with another and more importantly growing ourselves into a person fit for sharing in relationship we must know ourselves and be our best selves. We are fortunate to find a confidant born out of friendship who we respect, love and trust; so, do yourself a favor and be ready to meet them. Sometimes our immaturity or buried misgivings can prevent open conversation or dialogue with others and create misunderstandings.

Ignorance and lack of self-awareness can also stunt self-improvement and hinder closeness in friendships. Embedded insecurities compromise our togetherness. We don't trust the person in our life who loves us because of our past hurts. We worry that that person, will add more pain (one of the consequences of relationship too soon before healing or maturing). On the other's part, feeling or doubting that they will not be understood or be punished or marginalized if too much hurtful truth is revealed. So, we sometimes withhold information or are unaware and don't know of the baneful barge of baggage we are floating in our emotions is dangerous to ourselves and the relationship. Then circumstances occur that disturbs that island of submerged by-product of pain from its coma.

The pressures of life eventually awaken the hidden burdens and it explodes from its sleep, contaminating the relationship with arguments and mistrust. So true commitment is hard and hindered. However, if we are proactive about the positive construction of our character, our self-worth and emotional health; we will prepare and ready ourselves to present to our mate a more Spiritually mature person, comfortable with and in our own truth before we enter in the relationship.

Making immediate and positive adjustments in every phase and stage of our life, we can fix, repair and adjust issues. We can get comfortable with ourselves and allow another to discover the truth and enjoy the better you. We start with seeking God and HIS purpose for our lives and obeying HIS Commandments which are the road map to a wholesome, successful life. We must embrace HIS love and forgiveness. Follow HIS path and direction, be faithful and obedient to the Word, and HE will "give us the desires of our heart."

Trusting in HIM will prevent us from missing out on our blessings and beautiful people who are sent into our lives to be a beneficial companion and compliment. The life to good living is laid out in the Bible. Read it, obey and trust in its timeless and effective ability to guide and order your life. It is better to take the time to trust in the Lord and let HIM get us ready. We can begin by owning our sins and mistakes, asking and receiving forgiveness, redeeming our better self and commit to not repeating old bad habits and practices. Giving all problems to God, relieving ourselves of the burden. HE came to delivery us from our sin when He sent Jesus Christ on the Cross to die for all of us and all our sin. Receiving that gift, we can live a victorious life.

So, our start to getting ready begins with humility, self-forgiveness, faithfulness, love, deliverance, grace, truth, mercy, sacrifice and trust in God. Ready almost always includes (after preparation and study) a trial, a learned lesson and then starting over again after an accomplishment, mistake, a revelation or rebirth. We are never really finished beings, just flawed people preparing for a new beginning or level to complete a new journey or task in our growth to make us better, renewed and mature. There will be trials, tests and storms, ("to refine and purify") guaranteed. However, there is freedom in knowing Christ, HIS strength, Spirit and covering; will keep us through it all. Be ready when you make your choice to follow Christ it will be trying, troublesome, wonderful and worth it! It is rare that a married couple have a Cinderella© story, they met, they fall in love and live happily ever after. The reality is that between the meeting and the happily ever after, there is the decision and determination to stay together no matter what invasion or threat comes to their marriage.

That commitment equals hard work and dedication (from each and together) to face down all threats to their unity so they can get to blissful holy, matrimony. There is a commitment with each other to work together toward adjusting and aligning your goal; and divorce is not an option. Because they are one now, the two individually must loose unfruitful, selfish, unfocused behavior, desires and wants so that the "cleaving" that merges the oneness that is marriage is achieved. They live their journey resolved and steadfast with a practiced attitude that we know that we will succeed in our mission if we stick together. The two individually and "daily kill off the old self" to make sure this new union survives, thrives and prospers for its purpose.

They have defined and defended their purpose and adhere to daily working on getting ready and experiencing the joys of making their dream come true; a healthy, happy, respectful, loving, marriage. Happily living life, we begin the process of recognizing and resolving issues; preparing ourselves for the art (sacrifice and love) of getting ready for coupled oneness.

Introduction

ArtUReady? is a book to help us Spiritually look into our inner self and our most important relationship other than our relationship with Jesus Christ, our potential spouse. I am not a relationship expert of any sort or stretch of the imagination; rather I have discovered beauty in all the aspects of God's loving relationships. Included in ArtUReady? are these common views, suggestions, experiences, and thoughts on improvement or curious ponder (for most people) about relationship. Most importantly, the relationships in the Bible are presented and are telling and helpful today. They are intended to help us find your own pathway to successful relationships.

ArtUReady? is also based on an unusual outlook on some of the things learned about relationships, a reminder about some of the basics of relationships and a fresh look on the timeless components of successful relationships. I looked at the promise and power in relationships, extracted the good, isolated the bad, examined their health and cherish the benefit. I tossed them in this little book to share with the interested. I simply observed and appreciated the relationships in all areas of life; like relationships between and with neighbors, siblings, parents, friends, co-workers, and pets, those that serve you, waiters, gardeners, sales associates, etc., and noted the importance of love, honor, truth, right conduct and mutual respect.

To do this, I had to be alone with my impressions, and by myself to do some hard reflection, observation, introspection and growth. Then I placed resolute value on knowing what positive character traits I expected of myself and the treatment of and by others that I regard worthy and valuable to be part of my life. What does that look like? It took me back to the basics of the teachings of the Bible and regaining my moral values. ArtUReady? is my note-to-self, keep striving, remember and remind yourself to stay the Christian way and course. People you must have and naturally have a relationship with, can have very mean and selfish, self-serving attitudes and character, using them to attack you.

"The devil is a roaming lion, seeking whom he will devour (1 Peter 5:8)." So, don't be surprised or shocked at the person the attacks come from, the negative source is a spirit, not a person. Pledge to yourself that no one will violate your value, don't get disappointed by how well you thought of or how well you thought you knew the person. Allow not and don't agree (by ignoring) to ill-mannered folks and their mistreatment of you. Without your permission or unless you comply, no one can abuse you (unless you are a child and if you are a child, tell an authority of trusted adult right away).

Punctuate your life with positivity, fun events, hobbies and goals. There will be enough problems you create for yourself to contend with; without you succumbing to someone else's unfounded and uninitiated mean-spirited, broken, and dark disposition (bourn from their insecurities, jealousy and pain nonetheless, not your burden to carry) meant to try to disrupt your "joy" and to add to your troubles. ArtUReady? is a book to help us metaphorically hold a mirror to ourselves; so we can peer into our own true selves and physically into our own practice of life. To do that journey properly in life, we need to plan and prepare. There is a roadmap, the Bible. (Proverbs 20:21) "Many are the plans in a man's heart, but it is the decisions of the Lord that endures." "Write the vision and make it plain." Make sure your plans line up with God's will and plan for your life and your plans will be lasting. Take inventory of your life and let God prepare and shape you into the person HE designed you to be.

Focus on the plan of HIS intention for your life and live it meaningfully and "out loud." Receive HIS word as a mandate and don't let it dissolve into a mention. Others negatively interjecting themselves into to God's plan for your life cannot be tolerated. Remember who you are (a child of God) and pay thoughtful attention to staying on track. Rely on a familiar map of your personality, character and strengths to get started. For arrival to your self-discovery or recovery of your destination, pray, plan, act, and persevere. It is a part of the plan, that, most likely from your youth, you have had proficiency in certain activities or interests in academics that have come easy to you; coupled with events and circumstances (good and bad, spoken to or on you, revealed in a dream or vision) that have prepared you for your eventual career or profession. Additionally, it is usually fun and effortless for you or a (magnetic) draw you cannot ignore.

Remember and get to know your gifts and talents then blend them into the way you have fun or prefer to spend a fulfilling day and your career. Trust in HIM and continue to read the instruction manual, the Bible. HE requires your dutiful cooperation. So, holding on and remembering those truths, let us envision and paint a picture ordered by the Lord (Psalms 119:11) your purpose and developing resume will emerge. If the canvas is blank, what picture would you paint? Examine your wants and expectations of yourself. Create with limitless imagination; believing you can accomplish God's will for your life. Paint yourself Christian, moral and with emotionally whole beauty to incorporate into your intimate portrait.

Realize that God is directing you through HIS holy spirit, expecting that you will always, with faith, follow HIS design for your life. When you are the artist of your life, you must participate in the direction commanded for its success. Why, righteous provision is from the Lord. God is good and good is the standard to practice for success. Once every stroke is determined and mindfully placed according to God's plan and purpose, then you can enjoy how it looks and admire its beauty. I hope you let the Master teach you! Design where you are going with your life, and how are you going to get there. Lay out your tools, supplies, stay on course and pay attention to the details. Know that those quirky happenings and things are important.

Veering off course, mistakes, pride and lax behavior can cost you. In the world, there is the Father, Son and Holy Spirit and HIS Angels and there is also the devil his and angels. Dissect yourself and evaluate your entire connected family, friends and associates, and discover if they are a benefit or distraction. Know who lives in your world and evict all those unwelcome, unproductive, damaging spirits that seek to corrupt your living and destiny - no devils or demons in your world, out. So then, fashion a pretty, soft you and then style your scene. Would HE approve of who I am? Do my actions and intentions paint brushstrokes of kindness, love, joy, truth, grace, wisdom, integrity and perseverance?

Do I blend colors of education, charity, forgiveness and peace? Do I know my gifts and talents and use them to edify HIS kingdom? Spiritual (and natural) gifts are given freely (I Corinthians 12:4-31) are they showcased in your life portrait. People, with their gifts and talents will interact and intersect your life influencing your goals.

People also give gifts out of their abundance and the abundance of their heart (with love) to pour pure encouragement into your purpose. Advice, opportunity, money and referrals are evidence of your positive receipts toward Godly ordered steps. Without reservation and in love, give and accept gifts 'no strings attached.

Be thankful and appreciative of all gifts; share and give your gifts to benefit others as well. Jesus Christ is love and our gift, receive HIM and enjoy all the benefits of HIS love. I pray you discover quickly the love of Christ that I enjoy.

Decide, this "day whom you will serve" (Joshua 24:14-24). With guidance from the Bible discover for yourself, Jesus Christ, the Holy Spirit and Abba (Father), the trinity of everlasting love dedicated to the art of elevating our beautiful saving life and light, painting us ready. Ok, we both naturally, men and women have wants. What do we want? As you define your art in references of peace, kindness, joy, fun, love, activity, hobbies, career, Spirituality and purpose, attract the natural expressions of these in a friend. Art is their glue that joins their burning hearts and the differences, which makes the two complete. Beauty wants truth for companionship, but are you ready? Art is so subjective, so abstract, and so individually interpretive that a unique view is required for each person. Art speaks loudly to the right person. Are you ready to experience another's Art?

ArtUReady? explores a journey to find and refine your virtue; virtue which will attract the valiant man. Know that your inner peace, beauty, love and self-respect will appeal to a man who knows that family, order, protection, covering, security, provision and love for you is his joy and is the minimum he wants to do for you. He can, and he will conquer and discover himself, to mature; to locate and be joined with you. You decide if he is truly meant to accompany you in life.

~~~For instance, let's consider the growth of an Eaglet being prepared and trained by its mother for flight. Let's view the relationship with its parents, its environment, its resourcefulness to provide for itself, observation of its parent's instruction for survival and fortitude, its identification of friend or foe and its ability to follow instructions and learn. Its early life is dependent on its mother. Then its training and observations become evident as it strengthens and duplicates the example and influence of its father (mentor) as he grows. Now then, finally when the eaglet is strong and ready, its mother takes him out into the world and screams "fly." Because of their feedings, lessons and training, the parents know when the eaglet is ready, and they intentionally make his juvenile world uncomfortable. His parents know that he has out grown this stage of his life; there is a new mature world for him to experience and they push him toward it. Once he is launched into the world, from then on, every second of everyday the now growing eagle is maturing, creating, preparing and building his own life and future. His very existence is to stay strong, hunt, eat, avoid predators and traps and to scout for a suitable place to build his nest.

Then one day, instinct says to him "find her." Everything he has done to this point in his life has prepared him to be a mate, a father; to raise and protect his family and advance their journey in life. Ideally, a male child is prepared in a similar fashion. If he is fortunate, hopefully he has had positive Godly instruction to guide his journey into manhood. A toddler "stands up first on the inside" way before he starts to walk. All his life he uses instinct and fortitude to get through his next growing stage coupled with parental advice. He will learn through rites of passage, instruction for his growth, maturity and mentoring. His father will teach him the ways of the world and school will educate him balancing his life.

Humans however, have choices and free will. If peer pressure, poor examples, choices or foolishness enter his heart, his path can be corrupted. He either follows Godly parents who follow Christ or follows the world with its disorder and destruction.

Then one day, his parents announce, or the son decides he is ready and he journeys into the world on whichever side of good character or dereliction he falls. As this man enters or crosses your path influencing your world, you must decide to either date an ill-mannered son or date a readied man. Equally, we need to have been prepared ladies of grace and honor; and raised to only recognize and invite a fantastic man into our world.

If he is not right for you, run him off! If you know you are not right for him, leave him alone! If you are in process of getting right and ready (as we all should be) experience him now every day; in a friendly and familiar manner including his duties, interests and hobbies to get to know the real him. Observe now and consider how (in totality) his authentic character profile will compliment and complete your portrait. Consider and decide if he can join you in life's journey. Your casual interaction with him will reveal what he looks like on the inside, (his personality, spirit and soul). When "things happen," pay attention to how he represents himself and reacts in those moments. It is very telling, believe it. Take a general observation at all the relationships of this friend and eventually potential spouse; from how he treats his mother to the grocery clerk and mail carrier.

The ready man, like the eaglet has received proper training and wise counsel from a parent(s). Ideally, his instruction includes, a God centered home, a Christ filled relationship and regular study of the Bible. He prays. He "walks the walk and talks the talk." His word is true. He values self-examination and strives to continuously be a better person. He addresses problems and concerns the way Jesus would handle them, according to the instruction and lessons of the of the Bible (Commandments). He is supportive and helpful but encourages you to make your own decisions. He gives constructive criticism and information in love. He faces and handles his responsibilities and has an intimate circle of wise Godly friends that advise him on his best interests and he strives to be a gentleman and a decent human being. His conduct is revealed in all areas, under stress and in happy times (he should always desire to demonstrate self-control {Proverbs 28:25}). Some evidence that he values you (and himself) and views his relationship with you as worthwhile are; that he has positive future goals that include you.

He doesn't take advantage of you, your misfortune or exploit your weaknesses. He strengthens you and does not divide your heart, family or dreams. He lives a Christian lifestyle, be aware that the more committed he is to the Lord, the more challenging his life will be. So, remain a really good Christian friend to him and don't be a dramatic "millstone" around his neck" adding more nonsense to his life. Stay real and helpful, like him, (always clearing sin out of your life).

To him be real and recognize real in him. Just like money, when you study the genuine, authentic dollar bill, the counterfeit bills are easily identified and stand out as fake and phony. You don't even have to waste time trying to spend it, it reveals and announces its own truth; unreal, lacking quality, and worthless. Likewise, don't second guess the truth about someone, if it is an uncomfortable and a trying relationship that screams fake and unkind, quickly and politely get out and move on with your life. Not all men had healthy examples of men. So as a result, their drive for acceptance, affirmation or validation may cause them to make unwise choices. That care and concern should have come from a loving connected father. That lack of affection and training will stand out. His loss and ignorance are unfortunate, hopefully he is willing to improve and change for himself. at the top of their field (or game) invest in themselves with seminars, clinics, master classes, updates and the latest information and technology.

In his personal life as well, and for Spiritual growth, he should make the same intentional efforts to enrich himself. Likewise, it is up to him to take serious and value the romantic and relationship areas of his emotional life. Investing in himself for his future family as a husband and father. Taking serious efforts and painstaking steps to improve as a man. Ideally, he should ever be evolving and growing, your role is to recognize who he is and if he fits best in your life. If you didn't have a good father or a good example of a father figure in your childhood refer to the good examples of men in the Bible for your guide. Then revisit your choice of a companion and future husband to see if he is God's definition of man for you. Let him make that commitment and decision by and to himself to be what and who you need him to be as a man and friend. His biggest hurdle is admitting his need, after he comes to that conclusion on his own, he needs Godly male mentors.

However, if he is content with whom he is as a man and wants you to accept him the way he is, in (what you perceive as) his failing character and defiance to improve and change; kindly decline the invitation to date and move on. He does not fit your (Biblical) definition of a man, no harm no foul. Most decent men and women want mature, opposite equal mates, you are no different to require the best for yourself. Require a suitable, in kind friend. Unless you are ready yourself, you cannot recognize a man who is ready. When he admires your chaste behavior; counter balancing his sometimes less than ideal character you can positively influence him. Equally, be who you know he would want to marry. Before you meet him, be honest, beautiful, helpful, intelligent, kind, savvy, healthy, funny, flexible, Christian, hardworking, and agreeable. Both human and flawed be flexible, accountable and understanding; and in agreement strive to improve together. Enter the friendship ready to learn and grow. Examine your perception of circumstances and try always to see and extract the good from situations. Start off in the friendship cherishing each other and the relationship.

Like some of the funny paper dolls accented in this book, humor also ignites perspective into a bad situation. I think the "girlie's" differences are relatable and the emotions real. The girls are different on the outside because they represent all of us; on the inside, however they are the same. (Galatians 3:28)" ... All are one in Christ Jesus." Desires are common, pain is common, thinking is common, and joy is common. Some of the true awkwardness, dreams and desires of the dolls show our reactions, true thoughts or moments in our life. Take a pause to laugh at yourself through tough breaks, you are not alone. You are part of a community of people that experience the same situations you face, and you know they understand you. Have good girlfriends who live life alongside you. Be authentic, be purposeful, love, be grateful, have faith and enjoy your journey. Some of our experiences will be painful, unfair and unwarranted but eventually, positive essentials for our growth. These challenges, help make us ready. "Life is not fair, it is just," just what we need whether we understand it at the time or not.

So, avoid being bitter, unlikable and depressed. Instead start the process to fabulous and take steps to renew and rejuvenate yourself by appreciating your growth through adversity.

If you have been getting ready and don't think your counterpart is out there, don't lose heart. Come out of your hibernation and explore the possibilities and opportunities. Be proactive, be serious about your direction and adopt an excitement for new and developing possibilities. Have faith and conduct yourself in line with the truth of your promises. Not desperate or in despair "the glory is in the finish" so start the journey steady, prepared, ready and excited to meet (in the appropriate) a great guy.

Look forward to Spiritual security and Godly restoration in your renewed perspective and God will have your path cross your mates in due time. There is a beautiful world out there to explore. Great fun, satisfying experiences, wonderful times and real happiness to enjoy; have the attitude to claim your amazing destiny. We ladies are all a little different on the outside and every man has his choice, as do we. However, in general we all (men and women) want the same thing, love. After hope, trust, preparation, and action, there will be reconciliation. Come let's go get ready! I pray this book will be a blessing to you-enjoy.

My Happy

My happy is right now in this day

How I can enjoy the blessings

Happy with the birth of my new, to be, to obey

Pleased with me, striving to grow

Knowing myself

Happy to be with you now

By Ola Gilkey

1 CHAPTER
What is your dress size?

Dress size is just a metaphor for how you see yourself internally, (emotionally) and externally (your physical perception and observation of yourself). Sometimes we get discouraged about the way we look, rather than accepting that we are "fearfully and wonderfully made" by God. Thankfully that means that we are all fine just the way we are, despite us viewing ourselves with a condemning eye. In balance, your body is designed to serve you well through its intended life time, function and purpose. Despite that fact, we may not believe it and cause ourselves needless concern and harm by living a lifestyle unworthy of its proper maintenance. There is a duty to keep our body operating and functioning optimally, as it was designed. Sleep, water, nutritional food and medical exams, keeps our body healthy. Your body doesn't run on automatic, so its attentive care and maintenance is our responsibility and pleasure.

Lost and disconnected from Christ, we can get bogged down with life and temporarily not care or hurt to submersion so that attention to our (dress) body is just one of the least of our worries. Sometimes we get so distracted that we don't notice when things are sticking out. If your body is out of shape (don't feel guilty), get healthy and fit again, rebuild it and recover you. Remember though, your body is supposed to change with time, mourn the former self if you must, but let her go so the inner you (which should blossom and shine with your growing maturity) can take center stage. Let your emotions, spirit, wisdom and peacefulness thrive. As a compliment keep up your physical body in like order.

Going forward always try to continue to maintain a healthy body and lifestyle. Condemning yourself is not the right mind set to have, the right body for you is the healthy one for your stage in life. The now total, renewed you can present her true figure.

The healthy you looks different from others hereditarily created body, don't compare, be you. No one knows the true condition of stress your very pretty (dress) you could be in, except Jesus. The burdens of life, trials, persecution and challenges may have knit together a garment so heavy that some days you cannot endure its weight. Yes, it looks very beautiful on the outside to others, but no one knows the trouble it carries. It can cover a multitude of sins and hides a well-formed figure on a gorgeous being at the same time. The size of the dress is custom fit for you and you are the only one who can wear it.

Your dress size will change, embellishments added and repairs made and the Tailor (Jesus Christ) knows just what to do to hold your dress together and timeless. If you wear it with the knowledge of the Maker and HIS design for your fashion, the real burden which is HIS will be light and its health is a collaboration and tool for HIS purpose. HE will have you walk the "red carpet" in an haute couture gown when you trust Him with all. Be the woman you should be, a woman that God loves just the way she is, formed and called for His purpose and will. "He found her worshipping HIM, asking in prayer. He turned her around and made her ready." What did HE require to find her faithful, to be justified (what size was she?)? She was a sinner who had to repent, believe and she was saved. Get comfortable, you're in the right size.

The dress you wear sometimes seems inappropriate and gets dirty but wear it through the seasons. In time, this dress will be exchanged for a gorgeous gown. For now, there could be circumstances as to why you have a different body. Maybe you had to focus on a different area of your life for a time, so working out was a little less of a priority. Pressing concerns like having an illness, starting a new business, having a child, traveling, or helping a sick family member are all reasons your fitness time could have been distracted and hijacked from attending to yourself. Obviously, don't neglect anything that tells you that it needs attention, from change of shapes, to change of color or pain in your body. Irregular, odd, unnatural changes are indications and warnings of a deeper condition, have any abnormalities medically checked.

Remember, there are normal transitional changes. You may not remain the same size and should not retain the same emotional capacity throughout your life (you will grow, get stronger and mature). We all age and that is the bodies' way of saying to us, focus more on the inside and your zeal for things of Spiritual, mental, intellectual and emotional health and growth. With every new or changing shape there is purpose for transformation and adaptation. Your body may need to adjust to a new environment and routine; the shift/change could be to fit a new social activity, athletic achievement, or business profile. You're biographical and biological movement in life is girl, to teen and then woman. Your challenge is to pen, build, paint, innovate, fashion, found and live out your highest creation of your legacy.

There is a bridge we must cross over from youth to maturity, innocence to knowledge and circumstantial to intentional. Developmental female cycles are a sisterhood all young women share and pass through, so embrace the change and be ready to celebrate and endure all phases of your growth and purpose. It is great when a young lady is prepared through rites of passage training, designed to ready her to become a woman. She gains domestic skills, an education, a career and knowledge on how to relate to and take care of herself and her man (and eventual family).

She also reverently values the advice from older women. In that she learns to become a loving, patient, discreet, proper young woman. There is in this advice, advanced design to teach her to transition into womanhood. She is further blessed if she is a daughter raised in the home where a father model's benevolent treatment of his bride (her Mom). He knows he is responsible for raising her to recognize a husband (Sirach 7: 25 "Giving your daughter in marriage ends a great task; but give her to a worthy man."). Her father takes seriously his responsibilities for order, discipline, provision and Spiritual leadership. She sees who she should marry. She sees her mother's love, honor, respect, admiration and appreciation for her husband. She gets a balanced example of herself and her future husband in relationship. The bride's journey begins early in life. If that picture is not our story, then we must find our path to maturity and sound feminine qualities on our own.

So, get help, have a varied age and background of versatile female friends to encourage you and help you learn. Join a sorority, girls club or an international group of women. Have friends that give and offer uplifting Spiritual information and support for success in your life. Get counseling. Socialize with others who agree with and share your beliefs and convictions. With reflection and inflection, we should begin to feel and look good in your dress size now. Study women of the Bible, their character and response to circumstances. Like the use of salt, purify yourself. Proper behavior, restraint, good information and good instruction will help us to see ourselves as getting ready and awaken us to do savory, good deeds.

Permit yourself to re-train, plan, get some sleep and wake up to a new start daily. Move to another city if warranted to get a fresh start. Take time to refresh and rejuvenate yourself; spa treatments, hiking, swimming, yoga, singing, dancing, etc. Say and live self-affirming words and actions; and know you are beautiful and living a purposeful life. Turn a leisure hobby or pursuit i.e., knitting, sewing, painting, cooking into a helping project for others. Start a journal and believe in the power of your enlightened experience. Your social recreation or occupational passion can affect others in multiple ways; helping yourself and your community. It will also reveal and release your Spiritual gifts and that revelation is an honor and blessing to you. Your soul will be refreshed, and a business could be born. Feel free to refresh your surroundings or environment and (negative) people in it. Likewise, let go of the past and move into your new truth.

Whatever the dress size; it should fit (" numbers don't lie."). You are a Christian woman and you represent the "Body" of Christ. Your dress should be subtly flattering and culturally appropriate for your body. Get ready for your new self. Find the right health program for yourself, do the program the way it is supposed to be done, and you will create good habits to stay in your true size. Conversely, to discover who and what a healthy man is for your life, learn from respectable, upright uncles, brothers or mentors who cherish their wife and women. An honest Christian male friend will also share with you what he looks for in a mate. When an ordinary man see's you, everything in him that is a man will awaken.

When you provocatively dress, everything in a carnal man will stand up; and seek to chase and conquer you, gone after his conquest and victory. However, a Godly man that has decided and battled to put himself under submission (Galatians 5:16-24) to the Holy Spirit will turn his attention to truly getting to know the total you. He is likely to be attracted to a more modestly dressed woman that knows her worth. Self-assured, he can wait for the approval and the appropriate time to privately "enjoy" the rest of you in marriage.

I know it seems unfair ("life is not fair") that the more scantily dressed women seem to always get the guys; and even some men who go to Church or those who have "fallen off" their Spiritual walk take a 1st look at those women. However, the real proof of a man's depth of Spirituality and character will be revealed over time and in challenge to his patience to control himself. Your resolve to abstain from premarital sex will spare you from emotional peril when you remain a virtuous woman. Keep in mind, that not all women that publicly dress modestly are virtuous so both men and women need to be aware of whom they allow to occupy thoughts or space in their world. In the meantime, you keep yourself appropriately dressed and save the rest for his eyes only in marriage. Many of us have already made those mistakes.

However, take heart, forgive yourself and get back to the you that is on Spiritual course again. Be beautiful inside and out. If there is something unflattering that is sticking out, it is not normal for us and we need to heal or trim the excess. Fashion is sexy when you wear it and it doesn't wear you. Your real size inside and out is measured by your love and devotion to the Word. Get ready make it a fun size!

2 CHAPTER
What color should I paint with?

In your gallery are the emotionally endearing pictures of pursuits that complete your collection and it represents portraits of your total self. Your heart for giving, the way you cook for others, the time you spend reading to kids, volunteering at the hospital, sports, exploring fun vacations, drives down the coast, your book club with the girls, concerts in the park, organizing events, hosting an exchange student, or playing on the softball team; all are kinds of activities, pursuits or hobbies that make up the character colors you use to paint with that uniquely define you. You have adapted them based on their appeal to your lifestyle, desires, interests, "bent" and esthetic and they make up your lifestyle portfolio. Be happy with the blueprint for life, it is the markup for your gallery of qualities. Make sure even if one portrait gets damaged or broken that you are committed to repairing it or painting another one like it.

It is part of you and your vow to stay completely pretty, whole and authentic to yourself. They are treasured pieces and enduring parts of your life. Although your pieces may experience rotating seasons keep them in good order and repair. Apply regular rejuvenating touch ups where needed with ingredients of love—to stay museum ready. Every portrait has color cues and hues that work in harmony; when God innovatively designed the colors of your character portrait. HE also painted you with forgiveness and correction. HE added a heart of honest intentions paints strokes were placed to warm the design of your beauty. You are uniquely and wonderfully created, a truth of measure and calculation. Every pigment, every shade, and every highlight are a natural complement to your overall composition; as a beauty, a woman, a light. You must maintain an appreciation for yourself and others will see you as attractive. God made your beautiful, embrace and take care of yourself. Changing like a chameleon every time you begin dating someone new to fit what he thinks is his ideal woman, is tiring and wasteful. The right guy will accept and fall in love with the real you.

It may seem antiquated, old fashioned or unrealistic in this millennium; however, keep yourself chaste. Young women can start early taking seriously their virginity despite all the peer pressure and commercial messages that suggest "sexy and revealing" is the ultimate fashion statement.

Society doesn't readily show the back story and repercussions of reckless sexual promiscuity-disease, sterility, abortion, disappointment, heartbreak, or divorce. You see it manifested in escapism-drugs, alcohol, controlling abusive behavior, bullying and psychological problems connected to misunderstanding your fashion style. Paint your body off limits! Don't succumb to his or your lust and issues. "Your body is the temple of the Holy Spirit", protect it. Don't let a guy's flattery, "drag", empty promises or lack of maturity lure you into making foolish decisions that will corrupt and damage your future. Conversely, you may be the one "looking for love in all the wrong places." If you are a woman caught in the cycle of fornication, save yourself and stop. Take a pause to see your future the way God sees it, "blessed and highly favored." Then stay focused, on task and goal oriented. "Keep your eye on the prize! Occupy your time with worthy and investable memories. Talking to and knowing for sure, a man is your complement is truly fulfilling and sexy. Imagine how good it's going to be on your honeymoon night when you know the excitement is real, mutual and undeniable. There is a savor quite sweet when you have been waiting to experience and share this intimate moment with your husband, keep it special.

You will look back on this sexual fulfillment designed and reserved for marriage, with fondness and love. It is going to be rewarding and worth it! Don't get impatient, compromise or yield to temporary satisfaction at the sacrifice of your magnificent promised future. Repent and begin again waiting on the Lord. Just be yourself, stay on course and allow your mate to be attracted mostly to the Spiritually, sober you.

Maintain truth and integrity in all you do; call yourself who you are and let that be enough. Your intended mate will recognize you immediately and will be fascinated with the authentic you.

Otherwise, if you trade in your stilettos heels for flats so a guy who does not want you to be taller than he is, so he can be taller than you; you will eventually become annoyed. If you only wear sneakers, he may wonder if he is dating a guy friend or a girlfriend. If you try bowling and you can't stand breaking a freshly manicured fingernail, you will be resentful. If you like fine dining and he is super conservative about meals and expects you to cook all the time at home, you will feel unappreciated and uncared for. Be yourself and let the right guy fall in love with the real you. Color yourself okay!

However, do be open to his preferences and opinions. If he likes you in green, wear green sometimes to please him. Try a sport or movie he likes; you may discover that your interests will be expanded. It may be uncomfortable for you to try some of his likes initially, however; you might find later that you enjoy them. If you are ok with it, go ahead try it. Trade in your braids for a wig or cut your hair in a new style. If you don't like them, at least he knows you were open to try and he can leave you alone about it. Are you a "same Sadie or a mix it up Molly? Whatever style you are, you must retain your special appeal.

As well, nurture those traits you appreciate most and celebrate their value in each other. Nonetheless, keep your personal pursuits alive so that the real you and your likes can continue to be nourished. As well, enjoy the new hobbies, interests and suggestions he brings to the relationship that you have adopted. Ultimately, the picture of who you are is a most brilliant color when you style well your unique authentic pretty with comfortable, self-approved compositions and components. The man God has prepared for you sees you as alluring and your description just right for him. Consequently, he is attracted to you, not your material "stuff", superficial identification or influence. Be patient and resolved to wait for the right man who adores the real you. Also, you select a guy that you can live with ("figure of speech") right now.

Dreams do come true and goals are reached. However, sometimes tragedy finds its way into your life and the man you choose must be enough when chosen (hopeful and intentional expectations of growth from each other is desired and great, but there is no guarantee.

So, an understanding and awareness of possible stagnant maturity is wise. You can only be responsible for your own growth, pray for his and each other's together. Have a real time, present awareness of the knowledge of the edition of man you appreciate and pick. Take initiative to make the right decision initially. False images and perceptions of him are not reliable and can't sustain relationship success and support.

Hope in fantasy is foolish. The virtual guy is perfect. He never ages, leaves his socks on the floor, neglects romance and intimacy, cheats on you, squeezes the toothpaste from the "wrong" end of the tube, neglects your feelings, refuses to communicate or retreats to an internal or physically created "man cave." Don't get addicted to texting or social media and disregard personal contact and disregard interaction.

The real guy with all his habits, insecurities, financial problems, selfishness, disregard, handsome face, strength, caring, attentiveness generosity and charm that he possesses are part of discovering the real man and that takes time. There is no real-world refresh button for men. You can't truly "unfriend" him, delete him, swipe your finger, change screens, or easily walk away, there is history (emotional and connective). Know what kind of man you are courting and accepting in your life. Despite future setbacks, circumstances, challenges illness and problems every couple must overcome and endure; know, come what may, you still want to be with him. Rather than being wounded and blind-sided by his "stuff," take your time to get to know him. Your friendship and relationship should be in general comfortable and a pleasure to be a part of. However, there are tests and trials for every couple.

Be part of a healthy, growing and loving relationship building on a principled foundation. "The grass is not greener on the other side," so hang in there. Despite what appears, "someone is watering that green grass more and giving it more attention." Take care of your own relationship. As you know, most people who divorce would remarry their original spouse should the opportunity present its self. Stay home and "water your own grass."

Be fully persuaded that this relationship is for you and that you guys are worth fighting for and the task will be easier. Pay attention to each other. Let your belief in God's answer for a spouse and your agreement by your marriage to him, drive you! This resolve is made now while you are still single and dating. It is a mantra and standard you live by, then in marriage; it will be easier to "fight the good fight" together.

Learn in your singleness to be faithful. Avoid and ignore old, bad relationships and on social media, emotional affairs. "Guard your heart" and "submit yourself to your own husband" is a practice to master while you are single. Get to know him, some examples: know which one of these niceties he prefers while at social events: quietly staying near him, being affectionate toward him and/or making time for him. It is an exercise in getting to know and be comfortable with social interaction with him. Also, be mindful to use encouraging speech about him, speech that affirms him. That affirmation, should help you stay emotionally connected to him. Wisely understand and use your beauty toward your own future husband to flatter him and appeal to him alone (flirting with other men, can send mixed messages).

He should also show his care and concern for you. A quick phone call, or text during your day to see how you are doing; dinner or a stress relieving sport, flowers, your favorite activity, a gift or help with a chore will be a welcome display of his true concern. Helping you or giving you, good advice will also show you that he considers you his friend and he has a brotherly concern for your well-being beyond his attraction for you. Make sure he knows your unique way of feeling loved and connected. When these understandings, efforts and skills become second nature to you both, you are probably feeling, getting to know and growing closer to each other. You are getting ready for him as a wife, and is he getting ready for you as a husband. You will go through changes and transformations in all areas of your relationship. You can't think of everything that will affect your relationship. However, you should discuss the "big topics" the "must haves," "the deal breakers" and the "firm understandings of each's comfort level" before any serious commitments.

For instance, after you have birthed three of his beautiful children and your body has changed, it is not the time to hear and learn from him that "This is not the woman that I married...."

Of course, your body will change after childbirth, why doesn't he know that. Some women will get back in shape; however, most will never look the way they did pre-children (even with dedicated workout and nutrition changes). Do you both even want to have children (and share any known inability or childbearing fertility condition)? It will be sad to be ashamed of the man you married who does not appreciate the Mom you are now. He should continue to celebrate the woman he married after a life changing event (surgery, injury or disease). As well an honest sharing of current fertility concerns is his right to know; he will be hurt and scared if you hide that fact.

Certainly, when there is discussion of marriage, premarital counseling will save you both a lot of headache and heartache. Selfish, unrealistic and immature is a man who sees inevitable change as interruption to his idea of life and its affects. That is why it is better that a suitor has experience and have negotiated real life circumstances so that he can bring that skill set into the relationship. Put in the time to understand the character of the man you will marry and realize who you will commit to share your life, future and heart with. How pure is his sincere love and readiness for you? Both fully aware that marriage will be a work in progress (emphasis on work), get ready.

Once you are "in" be committed for better or for worse." Keep moving forward and work hard to get to better together. You are saturated with all the right colors for your family (paintings), right now. Live with your beauty, self-awareness and standards in place; then invite his authenticity, kindness, integrity and security to join you! The colors of his character will sometimes contrast, match or compliment your color hues. The maturity of colors transition with the stages of life, don't have in mind to change partners (rather, be flexible, grow, be ready to adapt, improve and evolve) when rain comes or controversy, resolve to weather the storms. Blue is an important color (him) and red (you) is also an important color; keep them both in vibrant perspective and balance.

Painting

When water meets color, something wonderful happens

An Artist watches the transition of the two blend

He uses a tool, the paint brush and dips it into their union

He starts a form to create the picture

The soothing liquid glides across a background of beginnings

Time progresses the shape, readying it to reveal the image

It releases its strengths, lines, shadow and curves to tell the feelings of emotion to birth the story

Flowing into their own space the colors follow soft directions attracting them to complete the painting

It is their destiny the combining of blue and red to create purple

A new splendid color, ready for renewed life as a new color

They enjoy, in time, sharing their story

by Ola Gilkey

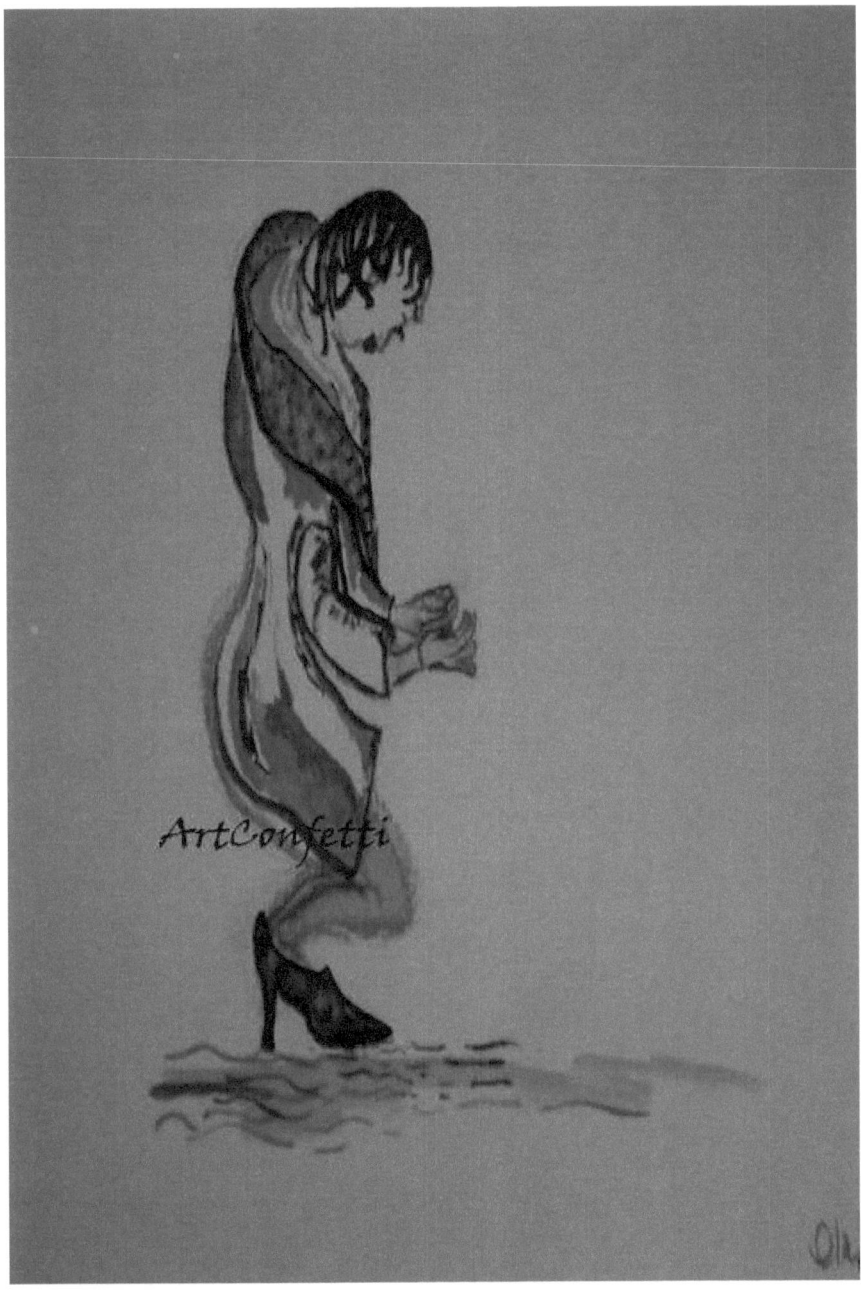

3 CHAPTER

Be a fruit inspector

Over the course of your dating experience, a variety of men will present themselves to you as a potential spouse. The truth of his character, will be evident and the consequences of his immature or ignorant (youthful) acts will also accompany him. His deeds, efforts and choices will produce fruit; you will recognize it as ready and nourishing or unripe and undesirable. You will need to discover their productivity to know that your combined efforts will produce a healthy harvest (together your life's mission; "Spiritual unity" and 'multiplying, increase on all levels, kids, etc. Take your time and only pick from an orchard that you know compliments and enriches what you have planted in your own orchard; and plan to grow and harvest into positive, fruitful accomplishments. Qualified suitors should expect you to be thorough and to examine the potential of your union.

Enjoy casual outings which will turn into discovering someone special who stands out. So, take your time and entertain dates and suitors until you choose. Just like going to the produce department, discover the fruits of his labor. Reputation, family, friendships, religion, colleagues, finances, mentors, mentees are all areas of influence on his personality. Find out what their impact says about him and his impact on them. As you gradually experience each area of his life just be mindful of the qualities you appreciate. Slowly, introduce him to things and people in your world so you can "know" if a sensible blend is likely. He needs the same savored time and thorough opportunity to get to know you and your character. If it takes a year or so to decide on the right house to buy, at least the same amount of time should be considered for a relationship of a lifetime. He should have ample time to check out who you are and decide if you also are right for him. Take time to discover him.

Does he believe in God, is he subject to God's authority, does he have a practice of good works, does he have fruitful business relationships, does he have integrity and respect for elders and others, does he worship and praise HIM, study the Bible and Pray?

Is he a caring, positive, Spiritual adult in some child's life? Does he have self-control, is he hospitable, fair minded, have a sound mind, does he know how to love you, is he honest, financially stable, truthful and follows sound principles? You should find him trained and training to face and beat the obstacles of life. "An idle mind is the devil's workshop." Idle chat and unfruitful pursuits will not grow him to maturity. "Every action has an equal and opposite reaction." Are his Spiritual reflexes acute to handle life's circumstances, problems and challenges? His readiness comes from faith in God, prayer, reading the Bible, a men's group, fatherly or mentor's advice and personal enlightenment by overcoming experiences. Is he patient, composed and level-headed in his responses? You want to feel safe in his leadership (servant hood). The real him will come out eventually, then accept him or move on without him. Period! Through dating, you are simply discovering compatibility, no harm no foul. Take the time to get acquainted with him. Guard your heart "a fool tells all that is in his heart." Get to know him first and verify and validate the relationship before you share the depths of your heart's desires.

Do you speak the same love languages (Dr. Chapman "Love Languages")? In the beginning, based on the little that you do know, are you persuaded to want to get to know more about him. Communicate with him not only in conversation but learn his language for love, recreation, religion, leisure, fun, games, planning, etc.

You need to understand the way, purpose and the definition of his life. If he says he is "crazy" believe him, if he says that he is "dangerous," believe him, if he says he is a "good dude," believe him (Luke 6:45 {truly what is in his heart will be spoken and demonstrated}). Receive the information and act accordingly. You might be able to handle or even appreciate crazy, but a good dude is what you should want.

Just make sure you know exactly what you are getting in him and choose wisely! Good or bad his actions and lifestyle over time will reveal the truth and if allowed, affect your life. Life's temptations, trials and tests will reveal his true character. In frustration, anger or pain he will tell you the truth.

"Whatever he says about himself, in word and deed believe him." Can you call him friend? Love is patient. How long does it take to get to know someone, a long time…? "Bring not every man into your house, for many are the snares of the crafty one" (Sirach 12:29). "Lodge a stranger with you, and he will subvert your course, and make a stranger of you to your own household" (Sirach 12:34).

View every kind of space you occupy and inhabit as your home, your private space only open to family, friends and loved ones. Define your emotional, structural dwelling, career, and physical body, as your "home." Know who you invite into your home and make sure they are not a stranger, covert bandit or undercover enemy, but a friend. He must first be a friend based on a valued and demonstrated commitment over time. He must understand and subscribe to friendship and have invested an established period of time with you through trying situations. Approve him on a baseline of friendship. Be thankful for the friendship and pray for him and yourself; that progress, separate or together will occur in achieving God's highest and best Spiritual elevation for your lives. That goal should be your hope for each other (Colossians 1).

4 CHAPTER
Set the guy free

He wants to please you but doesn't know how

He missed training from a Godly father, allow him to learn

He is afraid to be a father, his earthly father disappointed him

He doesn't want to appear weak to you, encourage him

Try to hear what he is saying, he is trying to communicate

He would rather run than seem incapable

He would rather lie than ask you for help

He would rather falsely pacify his problems than reveal them to you

He would rather pretend nothing is wrong before he confesses his sin

Be his friend and he will trust you

Prove him watching for blindness, change and production

Humanly flawed but Set him free from shame, the unknown and allow his heart to believe

If he belongs to you, keep him safe, protected and in peace!

By Ola Gilkey

5 CHAPTER
Is the doctor in?

(Ask all your important Health Care Questions):

Health: (Do you have any life-threatening diseases I should know about?)

Convictions: Yes or no? why?

Marriages: Yes, (how many) or no

Children: how many? (See above)

Mental Health: (Uh oh, not so easy, we all have a couple of issues!)

(Quirky habits, clinic stuff or medically diagnosed?)

(Sexual abuse, physical abuse, emotional abuse, etc., be informed)

Finances: (Debt, bankruptcy, school loans, alimony, child-support)

Spiritual beliefs: (Huge- "Don't be unequally yoked with unbelievers")

Anger Management Issues: (Short tempered, jealous, insecure, controlling; separates you from your family and friends; mean and threatening)

Addictions: (Smoker, alcoholism, pornography, gambling, etc.)

Other: ? (Communicate and talk to each other, at least know what you are getting into and make an informed choice)

No one is perfect, however there is at least one someone divinely created for you to enjoy life with; for you to grow into and within relationship with. When you are ready and comfortable with your friend and new companion, ask all the questions. Is he even available (a single man not currently married, in a mental capacity to pursue a wife, financially stable to support a wife, etc.)? "Dwell with each other according to knowledge."

Your marriage bond is sacred, put the time into 'discovery' while dating so that the future will be strong; based on determined fortitude and devotion to your sound relationship and foundation (now in the courtship so you can get to know him early on). (Ecclesiastes 1:9) "There is nothing new under the sun" all the sin; weaknesses, problems, issues, pain and sicknesses have always plagued our society. Lust and pornography are not new. Pornography for men (and a growing number of women) in our time is a huge problem. Beautiful women's images on television, celebrities and movie stars, have a team of chefs, fitness, health care, assistants and professionals who attend to their everyday cares and overall needs to make them look good. Their sole mission and job is to captivate men in fantasy. They have "up the ante" for everyday women, with beauty scales, while they still expect us to handle everyday problems and swat distractions, while looking gorgeous. Add kids, add emergencies, add special situations, and you are like-- what!! Meanwhile they can overlook their "beer belly," bad habits and bad attitude. In some men's minds, his real, beautiful, everyday wife is compared to the celebrities or pornography star.

In his distorted thoughts, his wife doesn't measure up (despite celebrity's air brushed photos, the benefit of surgery and timeless beauty frozen in digital and magazine format that defy the natural stages of aging). These images, allure and distract him from his wife who he truly loves. The displays are everywhere (conveniently and tragically in his pocket on his smart phone). In an unhealthy (internal or perceived) male competition to have the most beautiful women (as defined by physical attributes) some men fall prey to lust. Or as a diversion from realty, men fall into a trap of lustful deception that temporarily diverts their pain, masks stress or finds them chasing escapism. Then an addiction is created for those images and can include strip club patronage. That pleasurable scene is quickly a "go to" fix for all things painful or disappointments in his life; creating a cycle of indulgence, embarrassment and shame. They have mothers, wives, sisters and daughters, so they know it is wrong. Too weak and addicted to climb out of the "pit of lust" they hide, lie and surrender to its draw. They pursue the "other woman," desensitized and out of touch with the feelings of their real wife's emotions and needs.

Virtual, in a magazine or on a stage, it is still a betrayal and it hurts and can destroy the family. Pray for his restoration because he is lost, broken, and in denial, but encourage him to get help and in the meantime, avoid him until he is better. He can't truly commit to you if his "girlfriend" pornography is always first. To help fix the problem and to repair trust in that kind of relationship and to heal from personal disappointment and failure; some steps for him to recovery are to first, delete, destroy and remove all scenes and technology that they can easily access the pornography. Apologize to himself and any effected spouse, children, employer or friend; and admit to himself that he has a problem and seek professional help.

Pornography is costly in respect, income, and reputation, so any treatment is a bargain. It should be important to him to remove and eliminate it and its effects. The time and effort it takes to hide the problem and low self-esteem as a result, are all reasons that at any financial price, is low. Again, compared to getting a divorce or losing the respect of his wife, mother, children, colleagues and friends; getting help is priceless. (Daniel 13) "And Daniel said, "beauty has seduced you, lust has subverted your conscience." Men know men, so your man needs to get some help from other overcoming men as well or refer him to a Christian counselor or men's group for help for their overall health. Is he taking intentional, organized, scheduled, accountable and proven steps to correct the behavior, apologize, repent and give up the issue or addiction?

Things will look up (when they look to up to Heaven) when he becomes a more Spiritual, accountable man, then he can come back to you after recovery. He might need a men's group to help him feel comfortable to talk about his feelings and in a men's fellowship for prayer. He may need to learn in the comfort and safety from other men, skills to adjust, ways to navigate obstacles and tools for success. Don't look at the beginning, see the end by faith. You stay on your separate journey to improve. Get ready to heal, for the journey to recovery, to improvement, to understanding or to take the remedy of withdrawing from the relationship if it is not called to be or he refuses to get help.

If each determines that there it is a healthy relationship going forward, each submits to evaluations and discovers revelations about each other because they love you, love themselves and they want you guys to start out on a sound, honest foundation. From underlying issues to current health don't neglect the attention to know your man's overall health. It is important to know who you will be eventually sharing your body.

It must be with someone who has honestly revealed medical status and is willing to submit to medical examinations. Openly, know what each other suffers from and willing decide to accept the medical ailment or condition as part of the relationship. It could improve or get worse but be informed, (anger, insecurities and lack of self-control could be far worse, just know) decide based on knowledge. At least you are informed, armed and say yes aware of the total him; and begin living in the reward of truth. Give and request honest disclosures on all the areas of your lives that affect your new relationship. What seems is a big deal or deal breaker for someone else may be a behavior, action or disposition that you can live with. If he never improves, matures, "gets it," does it your way, or thinks like you; are you ok with him? This is the question you ask and answer yourself. If you are truly "in love" with the person, you will accept them totally. Be informed though and don't look back with regret.

Look forward toward improvement together and forsake all others (decent people should want to get change for the better). Other peoples' opinions of characteristics they think may help define your mate as better or wrong, is no concern of yours. You read and write the "article" of his affectionate, care for you and meaning in your life; knowing the whole story, dismiss all other's opinions. If you are a Banker or CFO, him having marginal financial skills may be a small issue. If you know with "your hands tied behind your back" you could easily manage the household funds, consider striking that shortcoming off your list. So then choose the characters you can live and can't live with. His lack in one area may seem minuscule compared to all his other gifts and talents that he brings to the relationship. Based on his total value, balance his contributions and attributes to your relationship.

If he lacks knowledge in any area he can take steps to gain knowledge and improve; education, job training etc. (James 1-5). You decide if waiting is in your best interest or your current stage of life requires accomplished, mature input and readiness.

Whatever is in our character will come out. If we are giving or kind, mean or jealous, insecure or rude it will come out. Our character is our gas tank of qualities or shameful faults. It is tested by weakness or strain and whatever is in our tank eventually spills under pressure. It is either a benefit or stain to our self, family, friends or circle of influence. If we are repairing ourselves and shortcomings, then we are growing. With correction, we can salvage ourselves and the relationship. Based on honest and open communication and commitment to self-improve and to the overall wholeness of the relationship we can begin again personally and together as a couple. Don't be critical or judgmental, work together to get better, if that is your choice. Get ready to take and give the truth and pay attention to any of the ailments.

Make sure you both are agreed on the destination, a foundation for an honest relationship, leading to an honorable marriage. Seek God in prayer for HIS will. Then, go slowly, modestly over time learning from and about each other. Hold hands until you arrive together at happy, don't let go, endure the challenges. Consider, before you throw away a relationship for 20% negativity and dismissing a guy with otherwise 80% decent character, (unless the 20% is atrocious). (Luke 5:31-32) – Jesus answered and said to them "Those who are well have no need of a physician, but those who are sick. I have not come to call the righteous, but sinners, to repentance." We can all get better, improve and heal.

So, show mercy so you can receive mercy and don't be too hard on yourself or him, we are all human and make mistakes. Keep trying to improve. (John 8:7) So when they continued asking Him, He raised Himself up and said to them, "He who is without sin among you, let him throw a stone at her first." All of us are a little off center, so weigh the malady and work first on fixing yourself. We are all sinners, so remember the importance of choosing wisely without condemnation, showing grace.

You are considering transitioning into having a confidant in your life, this friend must have and offer a little more than the average friendly acquaintance and a valuable spouse for life. Does he want a friend, a business partner, a wife, just know? "go ahead make your choice.

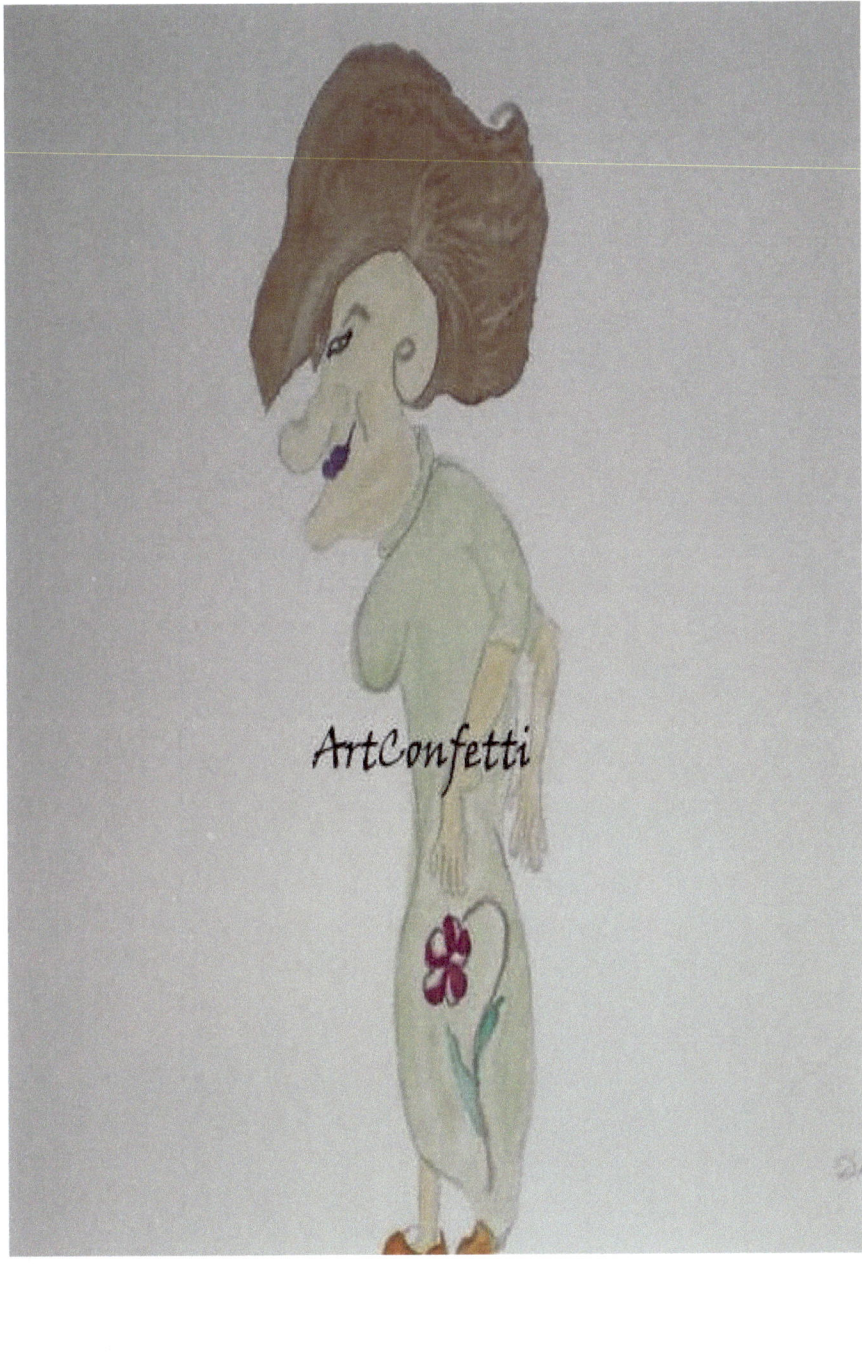

6 CHAPTER

Put Money on it

There are personal business aspects of relationships, that need to be addressed. Give as much weight and time to the business side of life as you do to the fun friendly side of life. Friends want the best for each other, and as friends a healthy financial strategy is approached equally from both partners and all angles. If you are a Doctor and he is a Gardner, then the expectation and assurance maybe is that both incomes are ideally viewed and recognized as one source, when married. That intact reality has no bearing on ego or traditional roles; it is just your family's income pool. The important aspect is investing in your family's future and those decisions are made by both of you. Have the money talk, decide and know the future financial specs. of your budding relationship. Is he a wise investor or chasing "a get rich quick, too good to be true scheme"? A Wall Street Harlot or Penny Pincher? Does he tithe out the first fruits of all?

Does he know that God will bless and multiply all his giving? Does he just give out of the kindness of his heart, the amount he deems appropriate or when he feels the desire to give? Who earns it; establish a savings account, account for special events, an emergency fund, vacations, investing, or his and her incidentals. Do you have joint accounts or both individual and joint accounts? Whatever the case, he needs to be a faithful steward with the financial blessings providing now and for his children's future and retirement. Decide together that the household funds will be a balance of managing, giving, saving and enjoying the money. Be mindful of a guy who is satisfied with you paying all the bills. If you lord over him harsh rules and consequences because you are the bread winner ("The golden rule" he who has the gold makes the rules") and demand his dignity for a price, you may threaten the order of the household. Are you okay with this being your future?

As you mature and reflect on his (non) contribution to the family finances, you may resent his continued perceived laziness. If he is comfortable being lax, he may lack leadership qualities.

He may see you more as a mother and less of a partner in life, shirking his financial responsibilities and duties to provide. Are you ready to sit down and create a plan to decide who is best or willing to take on the roles of your household that best serve the family and its financial mission? You may need to ("fall back") have less "lifestyle toys" or live a simpler lifestyle for love and allow him to work harder and financially support his household, if you consider that important. Sirach 25:1-25 ({21} "The man is a slave, in disgrace and shame, when a wife (financially) supports her husband.")—food for thought. Do you both have a common mission? Are you ready to listen to his ideas and give them due chance with reasonable support? Are you ready to change roles with the dictates of life's storm (sickness, natural disaster, etc.) to do what is uncomfortable and unfamiliar so that the best (financial) interest of the family and its members will remain preserved, protected and intact and continue to flourish? Are you willing to fight for the preservation of your union and daily do intimate maintenance to keep your world and family whole?

Don't get lost in the newness of the relationship, when everything they do and say is so nice and sweet. There will be financial times when he may need to lean on you for support or sickness that maybe debilitating. Are you resistant to that possibility or will you happily, do your part to maintain your financial stability and the resilience of the relationship? Tragedy and heartbreak will be a part of everyone's lives together.

In the middle of the "eye of any hurricane" (problem) try to free yourself of the stress with a fruitful distraction. Ride and pursue a different kind of swirl. It may be the last thing on your mind, however take a detour from the blues and move toward each other. Write a loving lively autobiography while this issue is looming. Divert attention to the intimate side of your lives. Let him finish the statement, you know I love you when I_____. Also, I know you love me when you_____.

It will certainly start a conversation to let you catch your breath and regroup from the problem. Let each other know if you are on the right path to pleasing the other.

Don't get offended if you are off base. See it as a call to action and use the information to nurture and attend to his other needs. When the storm has passed (and during if you are strong and coherent enough to be flexible and adjust to the times) this devotion to each other should bring you closer. Know for sure that his needs are being met and let him know how he can meet your needs. Be open, sharing and honest about all your desires and needs. Let it never be said that "I did not know that, otherwise I would have done it…" Carry currency of friendly love ready to explore the possibility of giving and doing to advance the relationship. You need currency in your account to spend it, so freely deposit and give love and grace so you have return on your investment. Use your love currency to purchase harmony. In harmony, there is built dignity, respect, unity, kindness, peace and happiness. "Hiccups" in life happen. How will you handle problems, messy situations and loss? Try to find the benefit or positivity in the circumstance.

Is he persevering while starting his own business? If he is ill, disabled, grieving from loss, temporarily raising the kids while looking for work or transitioning or reversing roles from a unique circumstance, it will require understanding. No matter the unforeseen problem, make him feel valued. His worth is the equity he is building in the relationship with you (maybe children or future children), during these trying financial circumstances by showing you his commitment and dedication. If he is continuing to forge ahead despite the problems in finances, compliment and commend him. Give him credit for trying to maintain his sanity while contributing to the relationship or family. Recognize and honor his efforts, understanding the total contribution; knowing that when the situation turns around he will resume and restore his financial responsibility toward the well-being of the (future) family. If he works from home, he is a provider. Be mindful of expecting a combined role as maid, chauffeur, entertainer, chef, and child provider from him, during his working hours. Most men inherently have a drive to provide and take care of their family. Find balance around and in both your schedules to address family household duties. Financial storms come and go.

When you guys are back to normal the attention to the building of the intimate side of the relationship will have flourished in that down time.

It will be even sturdier when times are better and you have done the work to extract each other's desires, wants and gestures of care. That attention to discovery will kick your relationship to an unimaginable level. So, stay flexible, encouraging and together. Be genuine about what you need to feel valued. Have the conversations, communicate, understand and plan.

7 CHAPTER

Out of order

(Truth & Consequences)

Stay together, stay attracted to each other, stay in order, remain satisfied with your present blessings and stay faithful. Define and know your expectations, keep the friendship/ relationship strong, together and intact. Let us examine men and women of the Bible who were disobedient or pompous (open your Bible, let's read).

(One "bad" apple)

{Adam and Eve- Adam should not have bitten from the apple.}

God gave Adam specific instructions not to eat from the tree of good and evil (Genesis 2:15). Eve had not even been made by God yet (Genesis 2:21-25)! Adam was with Eve when the cunning serpent tempted her "So when the woman saw that the tree was good for food, that it was pleasant to the eyes, and a tree desirable to make one wise, she took of its fruit and ate. She also gave to her husband with her, and he ate." God's plan requires order and obedience, neither one of them should have eaten the apple. Adam is the head of his wife. Eve is the "weaker vessel." It was Adam's responsibility to get between his wife and the snake (the threat) to first demand that she be obedient to him while he remains obedient to God and then remove the threat. It was the woman who was deceived. However, after Adam's breach of God's instruction, by eating the apple, everything in the world fell (sin began).

There are women in the world whose only intent is to entrap a man or break up a happy home (Proverbs 6). Equally, there are men that ruthlessly pursue their desires and wants, running over principles, women, and reason to satiate their lust and desires. A mother, aunt, sister or female friend are the first influences on a man. They will either display or impart in him positive or negative character, etiquette or dispositions of women. Know what kind of women help shape his beliefs ("He will treat you the way he treats his Mother.").

Is he kind to her, dismissive or abusive; or abused by her? She will inform him, deceive him or convince him that you are worthy or a hindrance and stumbling block to him. Decent women have an instinct to protect their son (brother, nephew, uncle, etc.) and "shout out" a threat to his wholeness, health, good name and dignity.

Don't be offended, when you are Spiritually grounded, whole and healthy; because those Spiritual women will recognize that you are a benefit to him. Relationships should be comfortable, so it should feel right, right away. Your potential mother-in-law (sister-in-law etc.) should accept you, value you and continue to hold him accountable to treat you well and respect your new family. More importantly, when he knows you are right for him, he will fight for you and against everyone to win you for himself despite anyone's opinion. Otherwise any female drama targeting you, maybe a window into his personal life. That is information for you to consider. Help him realize or recognize that this family dynamic and its "foreign" like influence on your budding relationship, may have negative effects, can be toxic or destructive. Speak to him about its truth. That wisdom in your character can protect you both when you politely share your observations and thoughts.

The information shouldn't be a personal attack against his people, just (relationship) "business." No matter where it initiated from (family, friends, relatives, etc.) negativity and drama is unwelcome and unhealthy for the relationship and must be eliminated. He may have never considered the behavior and its control on him (if he defends it, well then, now you know---he is not your match). Hopefully, it can lead him to trust, appreciate and recognize your ability to identify any threat and its origin to your relationship, no matter the source. It is what you will rely on also to decide if the relationship is right for you. Receive equally his insight on the negative influences and behavior in your life.

So then, make sure you know your man, that he stays strong in the spirit and has you in his heart. Does he know that not everyone deserves him and he is keeping himself Holy and wholly for you? Does he value his commitment to God and HIS authority over his life to obey HIS commandments which were given to keep him safe?

Is he strong enough to walk away and make decisions following Gods orders, despite you? Look at these men in Biblical times, their story is relevant today. There are categories of weakness that a man can fall into, in relationship to women and stewardship. These men all got out of order, but the good news is God gave them a second chance. They decided to continue to follow God's order and their destiny was preserved and restored.

("Cheat Notes")

Greed, mourning, loss of favor (2 Samuel versus' 11-12) David and Bathsheba [A King with many wives and the wealth of his kingdom looked upon another man's beautiful wife with lust. He had to have her and they committed adultery. He lied, he had her husband killed and he lost favor with God. It cost him respect from his soldiers, it cost her, her husband's life and it cost them the life of their son.]

("Unscrupulous housewives")

Breach, jealousy, loss of love

Abram, Sarai (Genesis 16-18:14) and Hagar

[The wife Sarai could not wait for God's promise to her husband Abram to give him a son despite his old age. She was desperate and "by any means necessary" wanted and was going to have a child. Sarai encouraged her husband Abram to have intercourse with her maidservant Hagar, and they did. Hagar became pregnant. The maid Hagar bore Abram a son (Ishmael). Hagar grew to despise Sarai and Sarai treated her harshly and Hagar fled with Ishmael into the wilderness. Abram was 86 when Ishmael was born. Abram was 99 when God renamed him Abraham and Sarai, Sarah (Genesis 17:15) (Genesis 17-18). Abraham and Sarah conceived their destined son Isaac in the same year. The cost of order to Abraham and Sarah was disrupted and altered. Abraham had two wives (baby mamas) and two sons, imagine the fights and division of interest!]

("Loco Snap")

Weakness, betrayal, loss of position

[Joseph was betrayed by his brothers and sold into slavery because his brothers were jealous of him. Joseph's father also favored him. Joseph shared with his brothers and father that God had given him a vision that showed their future service to him.

Seizing an opportunity to kill him, his jealous brothers schemed to leave him to die in a ditch; as faith and fate would have it, one brother instead persuaded them to sell him into slavery instead. Joseph was eventually released as a slave and became the Governor, 2nd in command of a great kingdom. He was trusted with King Potiphar's every possession and in essence had keys to the kingdom. Potiphar's wife grew in affection for Joseph because of his good looks and integrity. (Genesis 38:6-7 "Now Joseph was handsome in form and appearance. And it came to pass after these things that his master's wife cast longing eyes on Joseph and she said, "Lie with me."). She flirted and flirted with him, trying to seduce him. A Godly man, Joseph ignored her advances until one day she was so persistent, that he had to run and flee from her presence. As he ran Potiphar's wife grabbed and tore his beautiful coat. She used the coat to accuse Joseph of attempted rape and had her husband Potiphar throw innocent Joseph into prison. Potiphar lost his confidante and comrade, Joseph lost his freedom and Potiphar's wife lost the protection of Joseph's wisdom over the kingdom.] (Genesis 37, 38, 39 Joseph and Potiphar's wife).

{Also, consider the life of Samson in Judges 13-16}

There was some destruction in each of these bonds of matrimony. Read the passages fully and in context in the Bible. In the first case of David, he was in a prideful state; not satisfied with having it all. His greed was the beginning of his loss. In case number two it was Sarah's sense of pride that God could be forced to make good on HIS promise to give them a child in Sarah's time frame and not God's timing. In the last instance, Potiphar did not know when his wife was lying, neglected the true needs of his wife and left her desiring a young, handsome man. Potiphar's wife, doubtless a beautiful woman with everything worldly she could want, was obviously not accustomed to hearing the word "no" and pursued an adulterous relationship.

It is sure her pride got the best of her when Joseph ignored her advances. "Pride comes before a fall" (Proverbs 16:18). Stay humble in your gifts and always appreciate your blessings. Have a man who runs from the trappings of the heart, lust, greed and control. A man should not yield the leadership of his house to another, make sure he is secure and has your support in his leadership. Have order, agree to order and encourage order in your relationship. Be mindful not to try to coach him on how to be a man. He may resent even the notion of you tampering with his manhood. He may be put off or if he stays, he may artificially tell you what you want to hear or what he thinks you want to hear or superficially demonstrate conduct inconsistent with his true character.

Rather, take your time, the true him will come out, a man of integrity or not. If not, he is simply for you or not. Not your kind of a man, no harm no foul. You know what order, manner and conduct you should submit to in a man. Stay honorable to that Godly commitment and plan. No one wants to be uncomfortable performing behavior to meet the demands of a suitor for a partially fulfilling relationship. Instead, you both can individually be happy with someone else.

Don't be a doormat, lease your spirit or compromise your discernment. There needs to be a mutual attraction, decision to date and exclusive commitment to each other based on what is right for both and what you know about each other. Your culture, sensitivities and sensibilities should also harmonize and align with the intention for the best for each other and it should be evident. If you discover, he is not the one, no worries, it is not the end of the world. "Bad company corrupts good morals" (I Corinthians 15: 33). So, keeping your morals and principles intact, and move on. No worries.

Eventually begin a new (friend) relationship with another that is more naturally suitable for you. That new friendship should be more mutually gratifying and should grow based on your continual evaluation and renewal of yourself, each other and your needs. A relationship should be comfortable, natural and void of "recruiting" or "selling you" on the person or that relationship.

Empty promises of "I am the only one that will ever love you" is a trap ("the devil is a liar"). We all desire love and there are lots of wonderful people on this planet that want to truly love you. The ultimate love is this {John 3:16} "For God so loved the world that HE gave HIS only begotten Son so that whosoever believes in HIM may not die, but have eternal life." Another misguided promise, "I won't let anyone hurt you ever again." It may be well meaning, but often it turns out to be a thoughtless misstatement. We are all human, so the loved ones closest to us {family, spouse, children and friends} can be the ones that hurt us the most and worst. Unfortunately, as well, we can sometimes be our own "worst enemy;" tripping up and messing up our own best intentions.

Even if we had the worst parent(s), best parents or fantastic Pastor or irresponsible mentor, our (adult) will and decisions, are our own. We must take responsibility for our actions, choices and decisions; and not fault or credit anyone. Pain, neglect, loneliness, poverty, abuse and deprivation, of any kind, can be contributing factors and experiences to your station in life. However, no, not, as a child, none of it was your fault. However, don't let that define you. Be on a dogmatic mission to salvage your future. In remedy, as an adult, put on the full armor of God to protect you from new attacks (which will inevitably come) {Ephesians 6:10-18}. Change your mindset, success is a discipline. You or someone else could have easily made different choices under the exact same circumstances or born into the same or worse dilemmas in family dysfunction; and not have delved into the self-sabotage of insolence and ego. So, learn a new way to deal with problems.

Don't mask your pain with drugs, alcohol or reckless, deviant or defiant living or behavior. Our (prideful) sins will catch up with us and can be far worse than the initial problems or compound those problems. So, let's not get caught up in fault finding, "what if", "where" or "how" we started or negative ways to medicate. Start on a rebirth for your life. Absolutely, analyze the source of your pain or threat; remove it, heal, restore, recover, forgive and press forward, to the new you; but move forward. You will have new trials and troubles in your life (as we all do) and this preparation and training will give you new insight and experience to trust in the Lord to help you endure and persevere.

So, let's put blame, where blame is due, squarely at the foot of the devil. Know, it is a Spiritual battle between the Lord and the devil which is why you are a target. When you serve the Lord, seek and accept HIM as your Lord and Savior, you are Spiritual added to the devil's" hit list." He knows who is (or will) righteously serve the Lord. "Jesus I know, Paul I know, but who are you" (Acts 19:15). When you are serving the Lord, the devil knows you and therefore you are a target.

So, he tries to circumvent your efforts, success, journey and destiny by trying to destroy, dissuade and disappoint you in your Christian walk. He wants you to think you are abandoned, alone, forgotten, washed up, wasting your time or falsely believing in the Lord. Don't be deceived, your troubles are for a reason, so don't get discouraged. The Lord has a plan for your life, stay steadfast and faithful in the Lord. "The Lord won't allow on you more than you can bear" (1 Corinthians 10:13). "There is a way of escape." Stay clear on God being your Father and that HE will keep you and" make a way where there seems to be no way."

Although you may not "feel" it, you are protected and well able to overcome (in Christ) all the devil can throw at you. It is a fact, you are favored and in the peace, presence, power and protection of the Lord. Trouble, problems and issues will come to all of us, but HE has already won the battle, just cry out to HIM for help and HE will save you. Don't get mad at God and try to circumvent HIS path and directive for your life because you are angry and do not understand HIS journey for you and your life ("HIS ways are not our ways and thinking above ours" Isaiah 55:7-8). Trust and obey HIS commandments, it will turn out well "and what the devil meant for evil, the Lord will turn around for your good." (Romans 8:28).

Maturity comes from tests and experiences. Learn how to successfully pass, endure and navigate all obstacles with faith and trust in our Lord and Savior Jesus Christ ("Jesus is the Way Maker" {John 14: 6-7}). Don't compromise quality character, conviction and morals along the way to your future, goals and salvation. Rather, we must learn to lean, trust, and have faith in Jesus Christ and not get impatient, self-righteous or out of order.

So, continue to strive to govern and conduct yourself in a righteous way and forgive yourself. Look for that same effort and right living in other. Follow and trust God's will for your life. Not just hopeful, you should learn and know when a relationship is right for you. Don't be misled or disappointed by idealistic or unrealistic expectations. Stay in contact and connection with Spiritual family and likeminded Christians and friends.

Encourage and help each other reinforce your faith and convictions for the same cause; with fellowship in Christ Jesus ("do not forsake the assembly of others" {Hebrews 10:25}). Know the list of characteristics for a man in your life that God requires. Invest in (recognize, not involve in) and celebrate these manly characteristics in all the men in your life. The man in whom you will share your world for the rest of your lives, should emerge with these traits you have come to recognize and celebrate. Usually what you invest in grows. It is very important to take your time and listen to God's instruction and approval. Sure, we all have plans for our lives.

However, ultimately, God's plan is the best for us, submit your will to HIS. Have faith and trust in God ("the earth is Mine, and the fullness thereof "{Psalms 24}). HE is the boss, HE has the final say on our lives. The man he gives you may not look like you think he should look like but, remember "God looks on the inside of man." Be patient, you look to God and be in true peace with HIM and HIS decisions! "Every good and perfect thing comes from above" (James 1:17), you will know that it is right when it is confirmed that God sent him. It should also feel comfortable and natural. We have discernment, an instinct and inclination for knowing what is good, don't ignore it, embrace it!

8 CHAPTER

Ttyl

Test the Yen (desire) Loyalty {TTYL}.

You know your suitor, also has criteria, are you going to meet his needs? (Proverbs 20:14) "Home and possessions are an inheritance from parents, but a prudent wife is from the Lord." You really don't want a man who too quickly selects you as his bride. He needs to know that you are sent from the Lord. Holy matrimony is a loving devoted continued state of living. You want a husband who has weighed everything that you are, accepts it and confidently determines that you are his bride. (Proverbs 20:25) "It is a snare for a man to devote rashly something as holy, and afterward to reconsider his vows."

You want to be able to stand and count on his loyalty and dedication in all areas because his selection of you was wisely founded. You will be yoked together by mutual acceptance and endearing consideration. Your bonding is for life, know that you know, that you know, that he is the one for you. Trust also that he is sure; accepts you and is secure that you are the one. This is your life, be happy that he takes to task the seriousness of who he calls wife. A Chemist will remind us that for a mixture to optimally work you must respect and maintain the balance of ingredients to protect the integrity and intention for its designed usefulness. Are you there for each other and keep completely the elements of a wholesome relationship alive, balanced and well? Do you hold each other in high regard? Do you nourish equally Spirituality, love, personal space, health, intimacy, fun and adventurous growth in your relationship so that one unattended area will not weaken, disrupt or corrupt the balance of the entire relationship? The benefits will be preserved for years if we will determine to focus on the necessary balance and health of all the parts of the relationship as they relate to the functioning of the whole developing relationship!

We should appreciate a man who is proactive, intentional and who pays attention to this important part of his life. A man spends a considerable amount of time buying and preparing a house.

He wants a wife to help (mate) make it a home. Everybody knows this one, (Proverbs 22:9) "It is better to dwell in a corner of the housetop than in a roomy house with a quarrelsome woman." ("Proverbs 22:19) – "It is better to dwell in a wilderness than with a quarrelsome and vexatious woman." He is not going to live in a house with a woman that does not live up to his definition of woman and give her the title of his wife (to make his life a living hell). He will however, accept your past or behavior you may think disqualifies you as a wife; if he knows God approved you and he has followed God's instructions for his life and not his own preferences alone to receive you. He will be honored to have your calming and comforting personality to shine and share with him. He will know all about you and love you anyway.

So, be honest and real from the beginning of the friendship. "Let your yes be yes if you mean yes and let your no be no if you mean no" (James 5:12). If we cannot keep our word in small things, will we be able to keep our marital vows, oath, covenant or agreement? It will be an unstoppable truth that he knows that you are his "rib" when he knows and accepts the real you. (Hosea 1:1-11). The Lord told Hosea to "Go, take yourself a wife of harlotry, and children of harlotry, for the land has committed great harlotry by departing from the Lord."

In service, faith and reverence; when a Godly man listens and obeys the Lord, no matter what her figure looks like or her past deviant behavior; his selection will prove appropriate and suitable to benefit their union. God knows well beyond our limited understanding what it takes for those two people to make their marriage work. Trust in God's love and providence for you. Continue to be an honorable and dutiful friend in the relationship and let the Spiritual and the natural take its course.

Alternatively, your potential husband may have a wrong picture of wife or you may have a different description or prescription of wife for yourself and those ideals collide. So, for "Pete's sake" take the time to make sure God has called you to be together. He needs a helpmate, a partner, a teammate not an opponent or combatant spouse.

You equally need an honest, trustworthy, dependable man who gives you security in every sense of the word (including emotional, financial and fidelity). It could be after the courtship, that you make the determination that his idea of a wife is not Biblical and you could never compromise to pass his expectations. It is information for your decision. Based on your experience with him, personal guidelines, needs for improvement and confirmation for being real with yourself; decide on all the necessary elements for you to arrive at a belief if you should be together.

There is a beginning, middle and an end to determining your choice, don't prolong the inevitable, as soon as you know, make your decision. Caution, there is a "real time," limit to his evaluation too. He may have you on a "loop" or are making you his favorite playlist. If you are waiting or curious about the status of your relationship, you are being denied and/or in denial about the truth and reality of your relationship. Don't let him make sport of having you around and having things his way (he may have a comfortable feel good system going on that suits his needs and does not address your needs).

Be wise and know if he is stringing you along. He might be the type to justify wasting your time with excuses. "The measure of a man's character is what he will do when he thinks he can get away with it." Will your invested time be at your expense or benefit? Of course, he is not going to commit if you keep allowing his postponements to continue without expectations, examination or review. A mutual decision about growth toward and with each other should be wanted, warranted, feel right and desired. Everything in a relationship must have movement, progressing toward something positive, if it is not, it is stale. Do you want old, stale and stagnant to define an area or era of your life? If he is dragging you on year after year, you decide if he is ready to marry. He both needs to know what it feels like to be with you and get to know what it feels like to be without you. You both can learn the truth about the relationship by having equal time with and away from each other.

You don't get time back, and it is too expensive to waste! Some people make up things in their head, some listen to gossip and hearsay, some don't believe, some stereotype, others are just out of touch with reality or misguided by old thoughts and ways. If you have been authentic yet reserved, available for conversation and understanding, open to expression of dialogue and exchange; and you still get persecuted, challenged, neglected and misunderstood, just move on. "Pray for those who spitefully use you (Matthew 5:44)" and hurriedly get on with the rest of your life once you know the truth.

When you know, he is not the right one (don't waste his time either), get on with your lives. Cut your ties early and be thankful you examined your compatibility so you both can get to your ultimate mate. So, in that case, decline on the offer of continuing or lingering in a wasteful, time consuming relationship, he is welcome to be your friend. Your true husband is out there available to meet you, don't waste any more of your time on that relationship.

View it is as helpful and a learning experience that should hopefully benefit each of you; adding positivity, enlightenment and enriching growth to use in your lives and new relationship. Gain a new perspective for quicker identification of what is a good relationship for you and your life. Collaborate and cooperate with your ally, discernment. Trust, believe and be obedient, you will prove yourself wise, prudent and you will be protected. When God saves you from eminent danger don't look back (Genesis 19:17-26), keep your focus and life moving forward! Pressing forward into the next stage and level of your life, stay encouraged and in faith. Like Christianity, relationships and marriage is an exercise in "patience endurance and hope" so hang in there, your reward is great and benefits your destiny.

9 CHAPTER

"The flying Nelson"

In every relationship, there will be disagreements and conflict. Learn how to understand and address the real issue(s). Then recognize, manage and defuse underlying emotional baggage that may have existed and have been triggered by the fight. In self-defense add justice, use your knowledge of him to promote the relationship not tear it down. Look into his eyes and know you both lose if you hurt your friend and confidant. Our trusting service is to each other. We serve better standing up, shoulder to shoulder, side by side. Unless you two speak honestly in love together respecting each other's turn and understanding the other's point of view, any escalated dialogue, will find you emotionally divided. In defense of yourself, learn to fight fair "loud does not mean right."

Don't blind side or ambush each other with a "verbal choke hold" that you know will result in a man or woman down. Belittling, condemning, mean-spirited speech or amusement, at the others expense is damaging and unkind. As well, degrading words hurt, just like physical pain. If you share or express your opinion, are you punished, shamed, shut down or humiliated (especially if it is correcting, reveals mistakes or exposes lies) into allowing him to bully you into allowing him to have his way, if so, you are being abused and under condemnation.

If one side of your partnership is down especially because of condemning words and behavior (including passive aggressive "cold" warfare attacks: ignoring your text, talking negatively about you behind your back to other people (slandering your name with lies), intentionally missing dates/appointments with you, jealous of you, sabotaging you, etc.) you both will be missing a critical half of the team that could make the relationship vibrant. "It is the little foxes that spoil the vine," and the big ones destroy the vineyard. Recognize the behavior early on and eradicate it all. It is the beginning of destroying the relationship. What you think is a small matter may corrupt the entire relationship because of its compounding insults and hurts.

With no encouragement or praise to balance negative dialogue, it may open old, unresolved wounds. A wound that either of you may not have even been aware existed. Creating that kind of pain maybe hard or if at all, very difficult to recover from or repair.

Find out together how you can begin to correct the language, actions, mistake or misunderstanding. Are your words, works, and thoughts "kind, truthful, clear and necessary." Fortify the potential relationship by addressing the insecurities of the person "hurling the insults." Don't leave them lacking a thought of your forgiveness for them. However, require change. With devoted attention, by showing them just how much you love them with tender correction, they can change. Don't leave him weak, lacking or experiencing any void. If this one is a "keeper" but this area and behavior are keeping you guys far apart and you want to work on it and fix it; immediately invest in and investigate together (possibly counseling) the remedy.

Have no doubt that your relationship is whole by closing the matter with resolutely and amicably action. He will be considering you as a potential wife and how you treat him in upcoming uncomfortable and out right wrong matters. Your problem-solving techniques, your dedication and your respect for him will weigh heavy in his decision. So, for yourself and as general practice, regardless of any relationship, address any concerns rationally and don't avoid or escalate a problem. Choosing a wife is a monumental task that is crucial to the rest of his life, he must choose wisely.

Consider that if you were the husband, would you be the best wife of choice. You want him to be convinced that he has made a clear decision on asking you to be his wife. How ready are you? This man wants a wife ("He who finds a wife finds a good thing!" Proverbs 18:22). He needs your love and security. When he is weak, if he doesn't know and feel your love and connectedness, things like his decaying career, finances and naturally aging physical body may lead him into unhealthy behavior; cheating, drinking, etc., negatively affecting the beautiful balance of the relationship. Don't feel guilty, his weaknesses are not your fault, just be aware and avoid contributing to the problem.

If you are in it for the long run, the wrong speech or reaction could cause a deeper problem, you both will need to rectify. So be a good steward of the relationship now; and listen and obey your Spiritually moral compass (do the right thing to avoid trouble). Absolutely address problems, but don't be a nagging inconsiderate pain. Resolve conflict quickly and do it with a merry heart. Don't unleash on him verbal moves that land blows to his fragile ego. Start "cutting" him down with belittling words, and insults and you lose the fight (and possibly him). Then you will struggle to regain any sense of his love and affection.

Don't allow him to verbally or physically abuse you either in any way, there is no excuse. Men are wired to compete, so he will up the ante verbally (or physically) to covertly" win" by possibly cheating on you to feel some award-winning relief. "Two wrongs don't make a right." Resolve to talk about issues so that the common good of the relationship will be preserved. There are two sides to every story and being understood is each one's goal, right and desire.

An unresolved past hurt or childhood pain could be the underlying issue for an unsatisfactory response to what seems to you to be a reasonable request or comment but to him it is a big deal. Pay attention to the reaction, then note his response and discuss the intensity of his demeanor to what seems an ordinary gesture or speech. Help each discover, dissect and dismantle the problem or issue that has come between you, aggravating your peace and harmony. As well, don't let anyone make you so upset that it compromises your own decent character and behavior (don't go to hell, jail or your grave [early] for anyone). Just get out, when warranted.

Your endearing behavior, attitude and demeanor in talking and problem solving in tough situations is an asset. Keep your personality calm and focused during a crisis (and that comes with experience and maturity). A quality, honest "business like" attitude, processing emotions controlled; will be much appreciated and effective. Yes, it takes effort; intentional timing and a humble disposition, however, it will get positive results. Believe in him when no one else believes in him, be encouraging.

Make calculated decisions and changes together (with your union in mind) to work out your differences and to improve and grow together. "An ounce of prevention is worth a pound of cure." Please make sure that you are in it for the right reasons. If you are judgmental and unsatisfied with his behavior pre-marriage, most likely he and his behavior will be worst when married.

Work on the solution and resolution now and have no regrets. Otherwise, again, move on. Marriage is work, after the wedding and honeymoon; the daily tasks of two hearts continuing and communing in love begin. So, learn now how to get along and work things out as friends. Marriage is "one nation, under God indivisible, with liberty and justice for all." You will be on an island of holy matrimony; wed-locked and neither of you can or should want to leave. Marriage is a covenant, an agreement so your word is to the Lord. You don't just divorce your husband, you break covenant, your word with the Lord. Keep your integrity by preparing and then committing through all to stay together and honor your vows.

Yes, some weird things will happen once you are married and move in together because it is not your normal way of living and you are sharing your space with another who is espoused to his own comfortable living style. All his habits, rituals and behaviors are normal to him. To him, his way of doing things will be perfectly fine and ordinary, in relational stride, put it in context. You also will bring your unique personality and your normal way of doing things. Just be willing to get to understanding and to compromising.

Continue to love him through all things; they are most likely, just different and not wrong or unlawful, let it go. (2 Samuel 6:14-23 "Then David "danced" before the Lord with all his might; and David was wearing a linen ephod (apron)... ({16} "Now as the ark of the Lord came into the City of David, "Michal, Saul's daughter, looked through a window and saw King David leaping and whirling before the Lord; and she despised him in her heart. {20} "How glorious was the king of Israel today, uncovering himself today in the eyes of the maids of his servants as one of the base fellows shamelessly uncovers himself" ... {21}

"So David said to Michal, "It was before the Lord, who chose me instead of your father and all his house, to appoint me ruler over Israel. Therefore, I will play music before the Lord" … {22} And I will be even more undignified than this and will be humble in my own sight" …)}. Don't mock, be cynical or be sarcastic of a Godly man's seemingly odd and unconventional behavior. God has spoken to him directly and appointed him personally to perform a certain task a certain way. Although you may not understand his "Godly" actions, when you know that this man has been called by God, don't question him, support him.

In the best interest of each other and this new family that you will create, show support for him and talk about the concerns. The preservation of "togetherness in understanding" should be a top priority. It must be an integral vein in your prospective marital life source to stay together. Your first separate and intimate relationship with God is the only other supreme priority. "Unless the Lord builds the home, the laborers work in vain." If he marries you under conditions of; "my biological clock is ticking," "I am tired of waiting," or any other ultimatum, his commitment won't be sincere. If you guys get pregnant, he may will feel trapped and in the back of his mind believe he was forced into the marriage. He may therefore not abide by the obligations, responsibilities, and accountability marriage requires. He may instead and indeed long for, leave and return for freedom in his old life. If he feels only criticized, demeaned and feels inadequate, he will withdraw.

Instead, make sure you want him, the total him. Let him know and show him how much he is needed and he will feel loved, significant, encouraged, respected and appreciated. Examine and question yourself; I am making him feel like a man? He will need your support, approval and affirmation throughout the relationship to feel that he means something to you. Examine his true love for you to know if your investment is worthwhile and if together you both benefit and fit. There is added favor when you are in the "right" company (Genesis 30:27-30); so, stay just platonic friends so as not to" cloud" the reality of discovering compatibility and Spiritual maturity. When you trust the Lord and you both know HE has built your house (relationship) your joy will be full and the relationship blessed.

CHAPTER 10

"Phonie Bolognie"

Real Love

Does your love for each other look like this? I Corinthians 13: 4-8:

"Love suffers long and is kind; love does not envy; love does not parade itself, is not puffed up;

Does not behave rudely, does not seek its own, is not provoked, thinks no evil;

Does not rejoice in iniquity, but rejoices in the truth; bears all things, believes all things, hopes all things, endures all things. Love never fails.

1. Love suffers the ups and downs of the relationship. In those down times, love is kind and supportive. Love does not envy your success or blessings. Love is not on display or boastful.

2. Love is not harsh or abrasive. Love is for both parties (you are not in the relationship just to worship him; he values your state of oneness). Love does not provoke, it does not setup situations to induce circumstances to his advantage. Love thinks no evil (period).

3. Love does not celebrate in sin or wickedness. Love loves the truth and rejoices in honesty. Love carries all things good and bad in the relationship, knowing the glue of your love will keep you together no matter what.

Love doesn't question, you should already feel comfortable that he tells you the truth. Love hopes in all the dreams and all the goals you jointly and separately aspire. Love endures and withstands everything life throws at you. "You are either for me or against me." Identify your pleasant possibilities together and pledge your solidarity. There is no in between, gray area or halfhearted involvement. Rather, two hearts connected, exclusive, happy, intentional and freely united in their confident love.

Without question, you guys know you belong together and nothing and no one will separate you. To that end, please pay close attention to the way and manner he treats you. Alas, attraction is fleeting and like ordinary. It is true love that is real hard to come by and phonies and impostures abound. It is your responsibility to protect yourself and future by allowing only a Godly man and his proven love and the conduct in your plan for life.

You both should reasonably share the same love maturity and be in the same stage of Spiritual life. So, look at the "stuff" that could sabotage your relationship or have some negative impact on how you love him and resolve or remove it. If one is wealthier, more attractive, popular or smarter will you be able to acknowledge it and admire them without jealousy, insecurity or envy? Know and be satisfied with each other's style, educational and income level, talents, culture, and gifts, and be glad and comfortable with how they complement your own personality type and keep those attributes alive, pure and celebrated in your relationship.

11 CHAPTER

The Next Big Deal

Your guy, he may have good intentions, and it is good to have goals and a mission. However, in the matter of marriage if he is waiting for the "big (financial) deal" "to close on a winning project," to get that "big contract he has been working on" or "to finally make partner" before you guys can get married, how long do you wait? Is it an excuse and is there ever a guarantee that it will happen? Can you marry potential? Should you wait and understandingly support him? Are you on hold or has your pause button been depressed in the meantime? Are you a concrete factor in his dream or when the dream is realized, will you be part of a nightmare, because you were left behind? His career and occupation are a very important part of his life. It is reasonable that he feels good about himself and is ready to take on a bride after he has accomplished his financial goals and career. In the middle of making a way for himself in life he may meet the woman of his dreams, pause to marry her, or ask her to stand by his side until he makes it to his destination.

Your task is to determine if he is your future, are confident he wants you permanently in his life and you approve the parameters for your diligent support. Are you willing to invest time into a committed relationship or gamble on a guy whose choice, mind and goals may change later at your emotional expense and/or career? Are you willing to be on hold on to be with him? Whether it is to be the next president, build a space shuttle or plant the prettiest, healthiest organic garden that feeds his neighborhood; does he have a focused mission that also includes you? Will he be attentive to your needs and forsake all others (you should be first, not his job)? Working together, agree on the terms to the journey that will realize your collective dreams.

As well, have your career established and have room for quality time with your future spouse, if that is your requirement for him. Realize and recognize any unreasonable demands and stay flexible on changing speculations and time expectations. There are natural and unnatural events that can directly affect the "best laid plans."

Is it shuffling, coincidental or bad luck that alter plans? Is his word compromised or have recent unforeseen problems genuinely plagued his career or intentions? Many of us will have several careers along our lifetime, are his excuses or reasons. Make a wise and informed conclusion about the situation. Fact or fiction, know the truth about his involvement and place in your life. If he is important, your man should be a constant priority in your life. Drawing a relationship out, hoping this year will be the year, wastes both your time. Get past the "starry eyed" in love phase, because life needs to be addressed and the context you guys define to live it must be determined.

Don't make a hasty decision, our Father builds in stages and has HIS own time for scheduled completion. HE is still working on all of us, we all have potential and should be ever growing, so choose from your own heart and discernment. How does your life fit into each other's now and into the future? Be ready, don't toggle back and forth and play with his time or emotions either. Know your common mission and have the foresight to know if now is the right time for you guys to be together and to eventually get married. When you are ready for marriage demonstrate a "home" style and have a time limit for a proposal. An engagement ring is only a promise to marry, not the commitment yet; so, know and enforce your boundaries. Then once sure, be settled and prepared to take on the role and responsibilities of marriage.

Know also that your gifts and talents are his compliments and need to be used to support the greater mission. This mission must include provision for your care and his devotion and his commitment must be to you first (after Jesus Christ). Know your value, you have a price, commitment ("you are not on sale"). Let him confirm his love for you with a wedding ring that truly stands for endless, unbroken love. He should know what you think your life should look like; try to give you that life and try to offer more than you can imagine. You must both have the same agenda, get to know your man. (Ephesians 5:21-22 "submitting one to another in the fear of God. Wives, submit to your own husbands, as to the Lord."). Getting married must be a good idea to him! You are a big deal and worth it.

12 CHAPTER
"Phlatt Stanlie"

Has he been around yet defined by others? Embracing other ideas (even if they go against his sincere knowledge of right and wrong) to impress insecure peers; "the crowd," or misfits. Employing demeaning interpretations of women's needs and wants to fit in or be arrogant. Is he flat, laid back, nonchalant and is that your personality choice? If he is vague about his life and has not answered or defined for himself the mission for his life, is he ready for you? Is he submerged in past problems and afraid to move forward? Is he divorced and afraid of marriage or afraid to try again? Is he not sure he wants marriage in his future? Are you sure he is single and available? Do have some things in common? Are you comfortable with him or is there something that is just not, quite right? Does he have definite plans and goals for your future together?

Can he tell you what kind of guy he is, does he know that you are attracted to that type of guy? Does he have character to carry the duty of leader? If he is aimlessly wandering and not sure where he will go next, he may not be ready to share your life, unless you are also that gypsy type. Planning where his life is heading, may not be his "thing." He also may think that he is happy with you but after the truthful knowledge of himself he will realize God has a different mate for his life. Or is it that he may just need a little time to mature or realize that you both need to be equals and co-partners in life? His life choices should not be a game of chance, gaze or a glance look at your life, he should entertain the idea of and emerge with the conclusion of being "all in" with you.

There needs to be some intentional, focused goals and self-awareness for you to make an informed decision about any relationship. If there are many unresolved questions in his mind and heart, then that is for him to answer and resolve for himself. With communication, though, you get clear. By waiting a little longer to be alone and with himself, he could understand better how to relate to you.

Getting grounded himself should influence and confirm his peace of mind about being with you and any relationship with you. Building on his unique character and forging forward to meet his more ideal mate or blending his character and goals with yours to be a better companion is an answer he needs to come up with himself.

However, don't "sympathy date" because the guy is a nice guy. Have compassion and respect for him and let him go on his journey to find his right woman at the right time (or to realize his role in your relationship when the time is right) if he is undecided. Be a I Peter 3 woman and let your friend see his choice between a Godly woman and aimless pondering and pandering from relationship to relationship (collecting negative "heart ties" from each unsuccessful sexual relationship and the hardship and heart trauma attached to them.). Don't be a mark, participate in or let yourself be a target to an indecent man with lack of discretion, direction and meaningless appeal.

They have no problem hearing the word" no" from a woman, because they know every "no" gets them closer to a naive woman that will say "yes." He will victimize an insecure, weak, desperate woman that will prematurely say "yes" to his propositions not knowing his true character. He may also think that he is doing her a favor by" buying" her affection, addressing her financial need or giving flattering gifts (initially hiding his inadequacies). He may be relying on "auto pilot" having not evolved his understanding of women since his last childhood crush and has not discovered the flaws in his current dating style.

Habit, wishful thinking or relying on "what should work", (not considering the results; multiple, in kind break ups) are downfalls to his solving his dilemma. Not paying attention to how he negatively treats women, he is stuck in his routine. He may be just too oblivious to the investment, work and attention it takes to stay in a loving relationship. Naively wondering why another fabulous woman has passed, again on his invitation to date, share his plight or "opt out" of a monotone lifestyle; he repeats his frustrating pattern. It may" boil down" to his being resistant to change but change is inevitable and adapting and compromising is an art and part of successful dating.

Be confident in your value and say "yes" to only the right suitor that you will be excited to be with. Be thankful God spared you from this misadventure and concurrently imparted knowledge in you so that you can make wiser choices.

This practice of humility, meekness yet steadfast resolve to follow God's principles will help ready you for your future husband. Pray for him. Without appreciating and accepting the benefit of a well-meaning person's caring conversations, for them and about them; the epiphany for them will take longer to realize. If different people, in different situations keep describing to them that their character is immature and negative; and they don't heed the advice and pause to consider their ways and improve, then inevitably they will find "lonely" as a companion. Whether stubborn, insane or out of touch with reality the painful truth, hopefully will eventually set them free (learned on their own or through a heart-breaking struggle) to truly want a lasting, loving relationship. "Call no man happy before his death, for by how he ends, a man is known." (Sirach 12:28). Pray that he will reach his potential and arrive at his destiny of healthy wholeness and moral character. He will appreciate your prayers and God will bless you for pouring Spiritually into his life. This guy though is not ready for you yet.

With time, it will be clear to both of you when and if you should be together. As much as one wants to (through anguish) help someone (especially a friend) see clearer their misguided ways or mistakes, sometimes they bring on themselves difficult lessons that must be learned "the hard way." Until then, live your life "out loud" and have your fun. Just be a casual friend, loving your life and celebrating his decision to live his life, his way. If he genuinely wants a loving committed relationship with you, he will come around on his own. "What is meant to be will be when the time is right.

"Phlatt Stanlie"

Love him with Christ's love Accept him

Respect him Encourage him

Tell him Show him

Admire him

Congratulate him Support him

Desire the best for him

By Ola Gilkey

13 CHAPTER
Meatloaf

Meatloaf or Angus Beef? Corporate or blue collar? Country or Hip-Hop? What man God delivers and what man you are normally attracted to may be quite different! No matter his outward appearance or lifestyle image, recognize the right man. Have you dated him enough to know? Have you considered pre-marital counseling, a family member's recommendation or online? Have you asked your parent's approval or your best friend's advice to give you their opinion of him? These people know you best and a parent especially knows their child and has the importance of their future son-in-law in mind. Of course, yours is the final verdict and approval. You will live the day to day reality, joys and consequences.

No matter how you arrive at your decision be sure you select the qualified candidate, the man God has approved for you. What do you require from him who wants this beautiful state of living called marriage with you? A man whom you will live with within a conscious state of togetherness, harmony, fellowship, hardships, challenges and communion, must be special. He must be a friend, confidante, and partner. He must believe in the promotion of each other's mission for life. Get to truly know the characteristics you admire from this person who will share your life, your dreams, your goals and whom you are comfortable exposing your truest and deepest self?

He must be a protector, a priest (a man reading and grounded in the Word-Jesus is Lord of his life, his source for guidance), a leader, offers you security and emotional safety, a lover of your total care and a financial provider. Keep in mind, he also has a certain attraction, appeal and appreciation for a particular kind of woman. He expects an attractive, intimate companion, mother of his children, a nurse, caretaker, a chauffeur, cook, and maid. Are you willing? You are his helpmate. Are you willing to do all and whatever it takes to be at his service?

To commit to that kind of devotion, you must be in love with him, not just love him. A woman in love is the only one who will answer that call. "In love" requires a special spirit of joyful duty no matter what… 'What" is full of surprises, pain and glory, joy and anguish, fun and sadness. Don't take a chance or gamble on love, be sure. There is too much to risk. So, what do you compromise if you marry future potential, or have an "I will change him" mentality, or decide "his family doesn't matter?" You may risk disaster, you risk destruction.

Decide on marriage, based on his total character. Decide if his total world and disposition, including siblings, in-laws and all that is important to him is a good fit for you. Is he mature enough to "leave and cleave" his family for you? Are you ready to allow him to keep wholesome relationships, the ones that were a part of his life before you? Will he now include you in gatherings and considerations for group plans? Can he enjoy them without you but within healthy boundaries or limits, respecting his new relationship with you? If he never changes will you happily marry this man as he is and pray for continued growth individually and as a couple (in Christ)?

The beautiful balance of the home will be maintained when you often communicate and continue to learn about each other know and keep dear, uncompromising devotion, "forsaking all others." Talk to each other and find out the other's "love language." Are you speaking his language when you give him gifts, or save money or give him time to himself, does it say to him that you love him?

Or is talking together how he expresses love, is it sharing the same interests, or is it time alone to be with his guy friends? Does he like to be celebrated and have family and friends over for a dinner and fun afternoon? Is it important that you guys have fitness workouts together? Is he a reader and appreciates his quiet time to enjoy a good book or is he deep into "leave me alone, my sports are on?" Will he consider what you are doing for or to him, speak love according to his definition? Take the time to find out so that you can keep your love alive, prevent depression and create ever growing love for each other. Do you know what annoys him, irritates him, drives him crazy, or puts him off?

Ask and answer questions so that you don't "miss the mark" or make offensive mistakes or misjudgments and create costly misunderstandings. Get specific and detailed answers and responses. Sit down and communicate, which means you must attentively listen, then you can have productive conversations and dialogue.

Otherwise, because of lack of communication, solitude is what some men will seek if there is no connection. He will need and take time alone to understand his loneliness or to dissect the conflict, consider the answers and come up with a solution to the problem. A man's nature is to "fix things", that is what men do. His cave, of the mind or physical dwelling is his workshop. So, if you withdraw love, communication and affection from him, until he stops any of his bad habits or negative behavior and engages you in conversation about your concerns or includes you in decisions; he may hide or withdraw until he can compartmentalize and isolate the problems so that he can rationalize and the problem and find an answer on his own.

In the meantime, if the problems are not immediately addressed, it is possible that either of you may develop an unhealthy pursuit of the opposite sex for attention or approval. Self-medication whether chemicals or submerging yourself in other activity (sport or working) may take over his or your time artificially filling the brokenness. He will be looking for success, validation or achievement in the wrong person, activity or pursuit, corrupting the relationship, future vows and sanctity. Don't do it, "the silent treatment." Trying to clean up that mess and stay together, can be a titanic battle (if at all possible).

Instead communicate, in his world; that might mean playing golf with him, basketball, pool, bike riding, fishing or gardening. As you participate in activity with him and have meaningful dialogue and conversation with him, it will help him to relax and open to you as his friend, again. Without his and your input and sharing of your individual disappointments), there will be a lack of positive understanding. Without resolution, there can be no breaking down of the problem and it will get bigger or worse.

You cannot expect him to read your mind or expect him to know instinctively what pleases you either. If that happens, he will decide alone based on what he thinks his woman needs. He is not a woman, so he cannot think for you or think like you. He will use the same line of thinking that started you guys down this forked road; an assumption of his own creation.

You will likewise make compound mistakes giving him the "silent treatment" or "affection timeout" not realizing that that tactic is harmful. Don't assume that you know how he is feeling or thinking either, take a minute to have engaging conversation. Go play baseball, a video game, or bowling with him and let the conversation start and flow, so you guys can address your concerns and fix them. When two dynamic, intelligent, competent personalities are convicted on their way of doing things they naively see no problem. They are comfortable with their routine and lifestyle and their way of thinking.

They don't understand why the other person doesn't automatically come to think like they do and somehow know instinctively that their way of thinking and doing, is the right way. They don't enjoy the clash, but they fight for what is normal and comfortable to them. Differences don't have to be a declaration of war, talk and find the middle ground. These convictions, remember are the qualities you admired and that attracted you to the person, each should wisely and calmly use them to draw near to each other through understanding. They will use these same characteristics to defend against an outside attack or threat to you and your relationship, aren't you glad. You should engage in and protect the relationship with the same zeal of compromise and understanding.

Get on the same bus to the same destination; get along on the ride to harmony until you get it resolved. Both of you must come to realize that there are certain issues that require rules for collaboration for the two to continue to arrive at an agreement. Get on the same page, sit down and talk working out together the plan for resolution. After you talk, there will be a collective sigh and you both will wonder "why didn't you just say that in the first place?" Or agree to disagree, don't be divided (Mark 3:25) and put the issue to rest.

When you are dating, don't overlook or excuse obvious conditions or lifestyle. You are discovering compatibility; don't be oblivious to "red flags." Pay attention to anything that is not good for your relationship. Always keep in mind you will be saying to him, I you love "until death do you part."

Don't accept behavior or attitudes that are cute now but daily will drive you "crazy." Get to the bottom of issues, talk things out, solve the problem and/or compromise, make it a mutually beneficial understanding. Keep the love and respect alive focusing on the issue and its resolution. Have the tough conversations, what are you really getting yourself into. If he never changes will you still love him tomorrow? Is he financially stable, is he addicted to porn, gambling or drugs?

As well, turn the mirror around on yourself, what kind of person are you asking him to live with, are you the best he deserves? When courting, rather, express to him your desires and dislikes so he can get to know you, learn about you and understand you. Don't compromise your true self, "dumb down" or pretend you are someone that you are not to appease him in the beginning of the relationship. If something gets on your nerves or bothers you, tell him. Let him get to know your likes and dislikes. He is not a mind reader, let him fall in love with the real you or not!

When you are weak, if you don't know and feel his love and connectedness, things like trouble in the home, kids, bills, or work will trap you in a rejected, lonely state. You will need for him to pay more attention to you; date nights, talking with you attentively, telling you that you are beautiful, helping more around the house, and letting you know in your way, how much you are wanted and appreciated so that you can feel viable. When he does, you will feel loved, safe and honored. Has he shown that he can answered that call? You need his love and security.

Talk to, defend and share your point of view before the wedding so you both can learn how to negotiate and settle differing issues, knowing you still want to be together despite a few opposing concerns or preferences.

You each can explain your desire and have consideration for the other's views, without it being a deal breaker. You each have beliefs that will add value to your relationship, it is important to keep that sentiment in mind. You don't want your twin; you want to be his feminine compliment. Whether from family tradition, history or because that style or manner works for you, each person's individual opinion should be considered while devising an agreeable option that will be adopted for the well-being of your unity, mutual benefit and your subsequent new family dynamic.

Despite a negative history or well nurtured upbringing, determine to create a new family legacy that may blend old traditions and incorporate a more modern lifestyle for the new positive "you" (you + him=new "you"), that is right. You are becoming one. Have amicable resolutions and don't carry a disagreement over to the next day. The issue is now dead. Don't throw it back in his face later; take it through all the steps of confession, correction, forgiveness and repentance. Let it go (2 Corinthians 2:5-11)! You are experiencing and walking in the knowledge of what a Godly relationship should be, forgiveness and grace, stay on course.

The issues you face down together become less and less as you grow closer to understanding each other and grow toward a more ideal union. Give an issue a pause for consideration, give it attention, analyze the positives and the negatives, give it a conclusion and give it a funeral. Then, have a suitable burial and let it rest in peace. If it must, it will become a newly modified policy or an arrangement that benefits the both of you.

Otherwise, it has been mutually resolved. Be ready to talk through the problems. Be ready to be supportive, fearless, loving, protective of the relationship and stay ready to be there for him. Commit to stay together. Be honest and have mutual respect. Pray together and for each other and endure the obstacles and disagreements. However, too many arguments, in many different areas, unresolved and heated or uninvolved, lackadaisical, or unconcerned behavior is very telling of one's behavior and interest in the relationship.

One extreme or the other can be a sign of incompatibility (no one wants anyone too "clingy" or with anger management issues). Now is the time to examine the best for and from each other. Again, pray for discernment and do the right thing now as it relates to moving forward or letting go. You know and love yourself; you each desire equal interest, respect, love and passion from your companion. Don't let your ego or pride pick your mate ("Ah man, she is fine though" or being a "gold digger" and not paying attention to his character or being too young or immature to make a wise life choice.) Vanity is worthless. Life is calling, don't sleep on this opportunity for wholeness in relationship.

14 CHAPTER

Can't you feel that?

{Severe Cuts Anchored, Restoration Stat} - Scars

(A man with emotional and spiritual disconnection—He's just a friend, until he can know I AM)

A man you know can feel a very strong attraction to you beyond your looks. But to you, he is just a non-dating, non-romantic friend. He does not know the draw he is feeling for you is your anointed Spirit. He is not yet experiencing his own intimate relationship with our Lord and Savior Jesus Christ. He may already have some of the main natural Godly characters that make him a decent man. However, there are Spiritual qualities necessary for him to possess, to be able to be fulfilled and complete. Each person needs to receive for themselves, Jesus Christ their Lord and Savior. That declaration is personal and intimate. It is possible, that unfortunately, he does not know what a healthy interactive Christian family looks like or has ever experienced a Spiritually progressive woman.

You can demonstrate a life of Christian living and be an example of the love of Christ to him. Comfort his needs lovingly and caring as a friend. Yet requiring him to have increased positive advancement toward becoming a man called of Christ on his own. He needs to accept Jesus Christ truly (not just attend Church or say he is a Christian) before he can enjoy an overwhelming love, relationship with power (Acts 2 & 3) from and comfort in his Father. It is his task to aspire and desire to strive to be a better person. He needs to be a man about his Father's business. In Christian knowledge, he must take the initiative to learn how to be a Christian man. He now needs to just start and not worry about possibly the lack of a Godly leader in his childhood. Even though he is trying, be aware of any irregular behavior in certain situations that might trigger negative actions caused possibly by past hurts and/or immaturity.

If he wants to be an equivalent mate to you someday, he must learn the ways of the Lord.

With expectant patience, encourage him with each new positive step toward an intimate relationship with Christ and celebrate his achievements and desire to want a life God says will be "a life more abundantly." Help and encourage him to begin to move forward into the man God has called him to be and the Godly man you know he can be.

Start here → He needs Godly leadership in his current walk. Introduce or recommend he turn to a Christ Centered Church with a men's group. He needs a male mentor or male study group that follows Jesus' example. The study must be based on the Bible and the men's fellowship should provide a comfortable environment and relatable situations to help him navigate through unfamiliar and common distractions that can support his Spiritual growth. He can prove their Godly counsel by the challenge they place on him to do God's will and hold him accountable. He can nurture the growing word of the Lord in his heart by sharing and teaching what he is learning from the Bible with you.

He also needs to know and be allowed to be the leader in his home. He can learn how to share his Christianity with a prospective wife and children when he practices and indulges in a regularly scheduled prayer and study time. He will learn that he is responsible for himself, wife, children, and career with Spiritual covering.

His example, words and actions will set the tone for his growth in his moving toward Spiritual stability. If he falls, gets disappointed with himself or fails he should just demonstrate fortitude by continuing and committing to his journey to Christ (God is in control and will help him, he just needs to call on Him). He will also learn and appreciate leaning on and utilizing the support and wisdom from the brother's in his men's group and Christian friends. He will begin to learn his Spiritual way, know right path for the future and his journey.

Scars

He must be strong to survive an injury or wound

His scar is the evidence of his battle

He chooses self to defend and protect It is humble to "turn the other cheek."

But surrender no, it is noble to fight off attacks and pain

In what time and what circumstance did he have to decide?

It was his conviction that dictated the behavior

Observant, aware and stalking, sometimes the enemy picks him

A sacrifice for family, friend or person is why he engages the threat

We see the scar, we didn't see the battle, threat or problem A warrior or a scoundrel

We judge?

His wings fall off An angel disgraced and muddied

He is just lost and scared hiding from our gaze

We thought he was different (nah, turns out he's human too)

Sure, he is handsome and attractive on the outside

Yet, we resent the attitude, armor and lack of compassion imposed by his trauma

He is still in there, that decent man we suspect, struggling to survive and heal

He did what he thought best at the time

Maybe irrational, maybe warranted, now reflective-how to change

He has learned not to let "intensity" get him upset

A better way, preserve your dignity and destiny

Adjusting to balance the necessity, we are not the enemy, his spouse

A second chance anyway, despite …

The scar is there, it is his tattoo of humanness

It is right. Ready, give him grace and forgiveness.

By Ola Gilkey

15 CHAPTER
A Good Knight

Inside your real man is a good knight. A good knight has a decided journey toward his authentic headship and leadership! Recognize that he will need to spend some time with decent men that continually feed his Spiritual growth. Open space and encourage ways for his male relationships. He needs to be free to ask those tough questions and get real honest advice and answers without trying to impress you or appear weak in front of you because he does not already know the answer. He may need to examine his childhood journey and devise a mature plan by asking himself some hard questions that may require him to refocus his path. He could have some biological issues, relationship questions, father, emotional or career dilemmas that only another man can answer. A confidential male perspective can better help him confirm or adjust his journey. His positive masculine fellowship is part of his life that needs to flourish. He needs to find his own way utilizing great mentorship. A man needs to know that he is the architect that is building his own world. You help by praying and being a supporter (Proverbs 31). He may need male mentorship to help him answer some of his deepest questions.

Get to know his character and demeanor. How does he treat his women? Has his father, uncle, Grandfather, or Church men's group taught him how to take care of a woman? Does he open the door for the women in his life? Does he have a good job and is he a dutiful provider? Is he the Spiritual leader in his life, is he comfortable praying for and with you? He must discover the true meaning of "man" (mature man) for his life. A guy naturally needs to know he is the master of his destiny, the captain of his ship, and the dominant male of his tribe. If he releases that responsibility and choice to another, he will question the decision when problems arise.

However, when he makes it his own choice, he will stand by his decision and fight to make it work or take responsibility for the failure. A Christian man, knows his responsibility to be the Spiritual leader so he must spend focused time in the Word and prayer as well as fellowship in Bible study and Church service. He will then grow Spiritually to cover both of you. Allow him to grow without condemnation or cynical correction. Trust in God's order for HIS Church and watch HIM grow your man in the Word with you by his side (I Corinthians 11:2-3 "Now I praise you, brethren, that you remember me in all things and keep the traditions just as I delivered them to you. But I want you to know that "the head of everyman is Christ, the head of woman is man, and the head of Christ is God".)

If he was not raised in the Church but has later in his life accepted Jesus Christ as his Lord and Savior, you need to yield Spiritual leadership to him. Although you may be a stronger woman of faith and more learned in the Word because of your early study and training, encourage and let his leadership thrive. Pray for him and if asked, offer wise counsel. When humbly shared, he will trust you. He will validate the Word God gave to him and confirm the answer through your combined discernment, communication and answer from the Lord. Allow him space to reflect and readjust. Then enjoy the results!

16 CHAPTER

Concentration

There are moments in your relationship that let you know that the meaning of togetherness, life companionship or confidant is apparent in the shared moments of confirmation when you guys are together blissful and content. From a sweet note, a favorite song, a well-timed hug during a difficult period or challenge; you just know he cares and the comfort of your relationship is evident. Another sign that you are meant to be together, is that he should automatically and naturally come to your aid, care, defense and security. Commit to memory in your heart and mind words, smells, expressions or signals that trigger those good moments and precious physical keepsakes that will remind you of your togetherness and appeal.

Like the game of concentration, when the cards of life are turned upside down and are mysterious and silent; remember where the matching cards of comfort are located. The card for holding hands, a kiss on the forehead, the attention to your needs, the witty joke that made you laugh and took your mind off your troubles, the car ride to a more peaceful place where you could lose yourself in a new environment. "Think on good things" that are there to be turned over in your mind and used to be appreciated and cherished. These are the moments that allow you to remember the connection you have with each other, small reminders that bind your worlds together. Turnover and stir up in your mind sweet moments to counter act those cards that you were dealt that challenge your love, produce loss, pain, financial problems, or aguish. A private word in a desperate moment that triggers a sweet notion of his attentive presence can take you on a beautiful journey back to a tender moment you both shared.

Now reach deep into your soul where you know this guy is for you and find peace in knowing that you have found your best friend. Have covert names for sweet memories. Keep private and dear the touching concern for each other that will preserve your future intimacy and increase your oneness. Keep the integrity of your relationship intact by keeping in balance, unity through all pain.

Pray for each other and your togetherness. Be all in, be present, focus on the relationship and concentrate on each other.

17 CHAPTER
Living the life of Riley

Resist the temptation to assume you will live a carefree existence. The enemy is roaming trying to destroy your relationship with the Lord and your relationship. He will attack your worldly things attempting to disrupt your leisure life, professional life and health. As well as he will target your mind, body and spirit trying to disturb their stability. He is counting on your relaxed and unconcerned daily steps to infiltrate your life. The enemy is excited about those who are lulled into a "Living the Life of Riley" state. Haphazard, reckless living and that mishaps will make you vulnerable to all kinds of attacks, if you are not careful and alert. Don't fall asleep in life; keep your Christian life progressive and alert. Christian's are continuing to grow in their relationship with Christ. In that more Christ like growth, people disguised and envious will try to threaten your relationship(s).

With each new level of your development, the enemy is looking to destroy you. Despite getting tired of the attacks, you choose to go the distance with Christ. There is joy, peace and love included in your relationship with HIM expressed through praise and worship. From that will be your pleasure and desire to serve HIM. Oh, and then one day some event happens in your life and you decide to really love the Lord and obediently follow Him. You know and experience HIS presence and love in a very personal and special way, deep down in your heart and spirit. You surrender yourself completely to HIS correction and authority. You decide to reverently serve HIM, to make HIM the Lord of your life truly ('' Behold, "I stand at the door and knock. If anyone hears My voice and opens the door, I will come in to him and dine with him and he with Me. "To him who overcomes I will grant to sit with Me on My throne, as I also overcame and sat down with MY Father on His throne. "He who has an ear, let him hear what the Spirit says to the churches."). We are now part of the body of Christ!

Each one of us is a child of God because of your faith in Christ Jesus..." (Galatians 3:26-28). It is a wonderful revelation when you confess, accept and ask Jesus Christ into your heart and ask HIM to be your Lord and Savior (on a deeper level). You now know, understand and accept that there will be refining. So, God will begin to strip away people that are stealing your time and gifts. Unproductive pursuits in your life will be removed. Our selfish nature will be replaced with a heart of service and giving. Our speech will be of peace, grace and love.

Our focus will be enlightened on God's master plan and how the changes we went through were for HIS glory, designed purpose for our lives and our increase. He will burn away the negative habits and cut out greed and strife. A painful transformation will begin when we truly accept God to be the Lord of our life. He makes us more like HIM, into a person of valor, virtue and integrity. It is no easy task. The process will take us through uncomfortable, uneasy, unfamiliar and painful struggles and correction. We can accept the chastisement ("HE chastises' those whom He loves.") and correction when we know that it is to make us better; and better equipped to handle adversity. However, if we rebel, whine and question; we unfortunately get to repeat the painful lessons. In rebelling, we then also prolong the delivery of the blessings and maturity. HE will gladly put us back in "the fire for refining" repeatedly; or make us go around and around the mountain of disobedience until we get it right. A reconstruction of our will, will take place and "HIS will, will be done." Oh, but on the other side, "HE will restore what the devil has stolen."

We will become "a new creature in Christ." There will be evidence of HIS works in our lives. Our old friends won't recognize us. Curious folk will want to know what joy we have even during what seems to be a disastrous adversity or tragedy (and will marvel at your composure). "Our mourning will turn into joy" and "our crying into laughter!" Your discerning and knowledge will be turned up and fine-tuned.

It will be easier for you to recognize threats and rebuke demons before they can strike. You realize that there is a special blessing and favor on your life. Others will recognize it also and either their spirit will rejoice and be attracted to it or they will be very uncomfortable with it and will despise you. Either way, you belong to the Lord, be joyful and praise Him. HE calls you to love and forgive.

You discover by faith the real meaning of love. As the Lord Jesus Christ shared with Paul, "the greatest commandment is to have no other Gods before ME and to Love your neighbor as yourself." It is now time to make intentional wise change toward a Christ like life. (Revelation 3:19-22) "As many as I love, I rebuke and chasten." Therefore, be zealous and repent.

Be aware in even the small issues of your life, in common circumstances or familiar activities of your behavior and its consequences; you will be held accountable. Just because everyone does it, it is allowed, understood, and the terms and conditions are spelled out and agreed upon by the participants; you must still weigh and measure your conduct against who God has called you to be as a Christian. God is your authority. Consider if it is fitting and righteous to participate in what seems an innocent event or behavior. "When in Rome, do what the Romans do…" (Romans 12:2). Stay faithful to the conduct that keeps your soul. Be always in control, governed by the Holy Spirit. Stay on HIS path of righteousness and God will give those who love HIM a new reformed life until HE takes us home to Heaven. We will never be perfect, just in a constant state of improving and maturing. Everything you think impossible or hopeless, God has already made "a way where there seems to be no way"; to get you out of trouble, to save you, promote you and to answer your prayers, questions and supply your needs. You will be triumphant. Have faith in HIS word and rejoice in new strength and fortitude. (Isaiah 43:19) "Behold, I will do a new thing, Now it shall spring forth; shall you not know it? I will even make a road in the wilderness And rivers in the desert." "Kindness and truth shall meet; justice and peace shall kiss." We must live in thanksgiving and praise.

Thanking HIM for a second chance and praising HIM for HIS love and grace, as we journey on our "main street" and the "country road" to triumph. This is a separate, individual journey we must take alone. It is unique and personalized and custom-made journey tailored for our intimate growth toward Jesus Christ. It will certainly be a beneficial relationship that calls for the whole of your spirit to grow. "Greater is He that is within me, then He that is in the world."

That enlightenment will prompt you to be kind to one another. Then we will share our over comings and our victories with our family and new believers to give them empathy and encouragement to conquer their battles in their journey to come. We will help raise up a people who know the Lord and love HIM, and rest in HIS power. We will continue to add to our mission to "preach the gospel to the entire world," so that "whosoever will" can exercise their opportunity to receive Jesus Christ as their Lord and Savior. After receiving Jesus as your Lord and Savior you are saved by God's grace, nothing else you can do can get you into Heaven. Rejoice! Riley never had it so good. We are "Homeward" bound to Heaven!

18 CHAPTER

Wing Gate

Pray and praise through it all!

Prepare yourself to worship, praise, pray and hear from the Lord on all matters and all times. Use your natural way of praying. It could be a simple kneeling each morning. Just pray. It could be just saying Jesus help me. Moan in a minor key, just get it out verbally (Romans 8:26). Submit to the presence of the Lord, humbly and in surrender to HIM. You may have to go into a self-imposed hibernation, isolation, or solitary pray closet; mental and/or physical to get clear. Get a private Holy consultation, get ready, get confidence, get your answer and get strength for your journey to finish the race, from the source of blessings. No "vain repetition" of rehearsed prayer; (abandon insecurities, you are talking to your Father, unburden yourself) just pray how the spirit moves you and simply from your heart. In prayer, lay all your problems and cares at the "foot of the cross." Jesus died so that we may be free and redeemed, trust HIM and give HIM all your cares. Be astoundingly convicted in the spirit without reserve; sincerely and reverently talking to and listening to the Holy Spirit, intimately. Enter prayer with thanksgiving and praise. Just be alone and present with the Lord or in agreement in prayer with other prayer partners. Pray according to HIS will. Be open and submitted, bringing your prayers and requests to the Lord.

If need be, have written down your vision, goals, problem, challenge, question or request. You will see in writing what you already know, that only that which is according to HIS will, will be done. You can see any requests that would not be pleasing to HIS purpose for your life. That exercise alone should help you eliminate what you know God will not honor, bless or grant. The Bible is the rule book for right living, consult it and live by and trust in the Lord. HE will answer you according to His Word, "My sheep hear my voice"! Don't try to interpret HIS answer or question HIS time frame ("HIS ways are not our ways, they are above our thinking and understanding").

His way and Word is sufficient to provide and protect you (the Lord's prayer-Matthew 6:9-13). Be attentive to hear HIS Word.

Get closer to HIM after purging from sin, asking for forgiveness and fasting. We must be a prepared vessel, with a right spirit, open and ready to receive God's coming answers to our prayers. If not for yourself, for the loved ones in our lives, we need to be in right standing with God to get an intercessory pray through to God on others behave. Have also prayer partners to cover your weaknesses. Take note, HE only hears a righteous man or woman. "The prayers of a righteous man availeth much" (James 5:13-19). "Be a tree planted by the rivers of waters" (Psalms 1:3). So be a person trying to do right; with solid, deep, nutrient rich roots in the Word that transports blessings to loved ones in your family tree because you are firmly planted in the Word of God.

Pray for your coming spouse, yourself, your marriage and everyone that has influence on you. After you pray, be patient. God's timing is HIS own and may seem like an eternity to us. But to God it is perfect timing. HE is making you ready, fixing the problem or preparing the blessing you prayed for. He is timing the delivery of the answer just right for your ability to take care of it, appreciate it or getting someone out of your way or your life that may destroy it intentionally or unintentionally.

In the meantime, live your life merrily in praise, thanksgiving and with joy; focused on being like Jesus. Stir your desire. Don't lose heart; God will answer your prayer, keep praying (Luke 11:1-4). God's measure of time is not our measure of time. God's soon may be 10 years or longer for us. During this time in your life, stay Spiritually healthy, grounded and in training to be ready to receive your blessings. If a husband is on your prayer list, that request could take time or a quick granting. Either way, we are a fallen people needing to be put back together. So be patient and joyful in either deliverance. Your mate will most likely find you praying, working or sharing the same interests or common space. You do the same, stay in the Word, stay busy and enjoy life. We pray he is praying for you like you are praying for him, and in the activity of life, the Father will arrange for you to meet.

You want your Adam (husband) formed and readied by the Creator who is excited to be with you. (Genesis 2:24-25 "Therefore a man shall leave his father and mother and be joined to his wife, and they shall become one flesh. And they were both naked, the man and his wife, and were not shamed.") He needs to be a Spiritually mature man (I Corinthians 13:11) who will be capable of leaving his family of origin, to birth his own new family with you.

He needs to be willing to provide for you and have a discernment and ability to totally take care of his family. He needs to be emotionally naked, transparent, and open with his wife in a wholly committed relationship that is "until death do we part" and sacred from all others. You are a master piece charged with the duty of taking care of another master piece. (Malachi 2:16 "God the Lord God of Israel says that He hates divorce…). You will be one spirit, united in one body, working toward one unified mission (husband and wife). Make all decisions based on the Word of God together with the art of husbandry :), your calling. Take the time, develop and get to know yourself, get to know each other and wisely wait on God. There are a lot of men you can have an ok relationship with. However, there is at least one-man God called to be your husband that you can have an amazing marital relationship. If you are willing to wait for him, now you are ready.

Ready is a continued state of preparation for new levels. In patient peace, embrace and address with love, your destiny and new challenges in meeting him. You are not capable of or expected to know everything about a relationship nor should you be paranoid or impose tactics and make up scenarios to combat or worry about, in preparation for one. "What if" possibilities and situations created in trying to analyze a relationship only create mistrust and insecurities. However, you should diligently position, develop, take time, know and Spiritually ready yourself before you enter a relationship. Trust your discernments and instinct; and enjoy the forecast of a pleasant experience.

You are ready if you have chosen someone who will die for you and he will live for you. He will live to honor you, to love you, to give you security and to give you his trust and heart. He will live to give you a healthy lifestyle and to meet your every need.

Through challenge and peace, he is ready to die to self and to die for you. I only know one person that is totally devoted and completely capable of meeting all those desires, Jesus Christ. So, you are truly ready when our Father who are in Heaven is your first love and King! God will not accept you having "any other God's before HIM." No man, no husband, no idol, no hero, no child, no hobby, no job, no family member or celebrity; before HIM (Matthew 4:10). We are pursuing ready when we know "the fear of the lord is the beginning of wisdom." You are ready when you learn to lean on the Lord for everything! HE is the only one who can fulfill all your needs (Philippians 4:19).

A man is human and will make mistakes, he will disappoint you and he will fail sometimes and hurt you (you as well, so be ready to forgive, have grace and have compassion). Be in praise and thanksgiving; Jesus has already come to be your husband ("the Church is the Bride of Christ"). If it is God's will for you to be married, you will be. Just let HIM bring you to your earthly husband. At the appointed time, it will go well, relax.

Perhaps

Today Perhaps today maybe the day you realize you

Perhaps today maybe the day you meet him

Perhaps today maybe the day you know the truth

Perhaps today maybe the day you accept the plan

Perhaps today maybe the day your fruit grows

Perhaps today maybe the day the maturity blossoms

Perhaps today is the day you must be ready

Perhaps today maybe the day our Savior comes

By Ola Gilkey

Be Ready

To ask HIM for help

To unburden yourself

To ask for forgiveness

To ask for direction

To lean on HIS shoulders

To cry in HIS comfort

To rest in HIS love

To live in HIS blessings

By Ola Gilkey

From THE AUTHOR

ArtUReady? is written to encourage us to pursue our desires, dreams and destiny, through Jesus Christ. I am a woman, who is living her life in revitalized revelation, while waiting and growing through all life has in store for me. A single woman, I enjoy pursuits like eclectic art, sports, dancing and dining. Creative writing has shaped my world and sparked my thirst to be optimistic about life and explore its wonders. Like some other ordinary people, I am not particularly trained, academically educated or learned about the Bible; but somehow God saw fit to write through me the message of this book.

Likewise, I pray you look not to the world for approval but to follow the prompting of the Holy Spirit by faith, hope and commitment, to pursue and finish the assignment God has given you. I know you can accomplish it, God has given you all the tools you need and the requisite suffering, understanding, blessings, experience and appreciation to make it happen. Proverbs 24:16 "For the just man falls seven times and rises again, but the wicked stumble to ruin."

Don't look at your past mistakes; keep your eyes on the plan and vision for your future staying on the right path. There is a way to "redeem the days the locust has destroyed" trust and have faith in Jesus Christ. (1 Corinthians 1-2:5). "Consequently, your faith rests not on the wisdom of men but on the power of God. "Receive God as the Lord and Savior of your life and watch the "unthinkable and imaginable" happen. ArtUReady? is my way to encourage you to live your life with faith in Jesus Christ. Invest time and study the Word and the things that make you happy and that make you a better person, will emerge. Get ready to fulfill the call and mission for your life.

Our Father will tell you, instruct you, go before you and be with you (Joshua 1) to accomplish your goals. God is working on your behalf. You can't always see His construction; just trust in Him, be obedient and have faith you will succeed. In each ordinary day of your life, there is an opportunity to meet your husband at work or play, and to benefit from his companionship. We want a mate to share the journey. You are never more satisfied than when you have a husband by your side who loves the best of you despite the worst of you.

He by far is not your everything; but an intentional part of God's plan for HIS children to live life coupled. Be joyful and grounded in Christ first. I hope you discover your mate praying for you and I hope he discovers you happily praying for him too. I hope the Lord shines on your union. I hope you are ready for the next phase of your life.

Thank you for purchasing this book. Daniel's Friends and Dogmatic Doggie Days are two of our other popular books coming soon that you may enjoy. "ArtConfetti, is where a world of beautiful, eclectic pieces of art bloom to celebrate and decorate your life!" ®. Please visit our website at ArtConfetti.com ©® for a festive selection of beautiful books, t-shirts and greeting cards.

Minuet

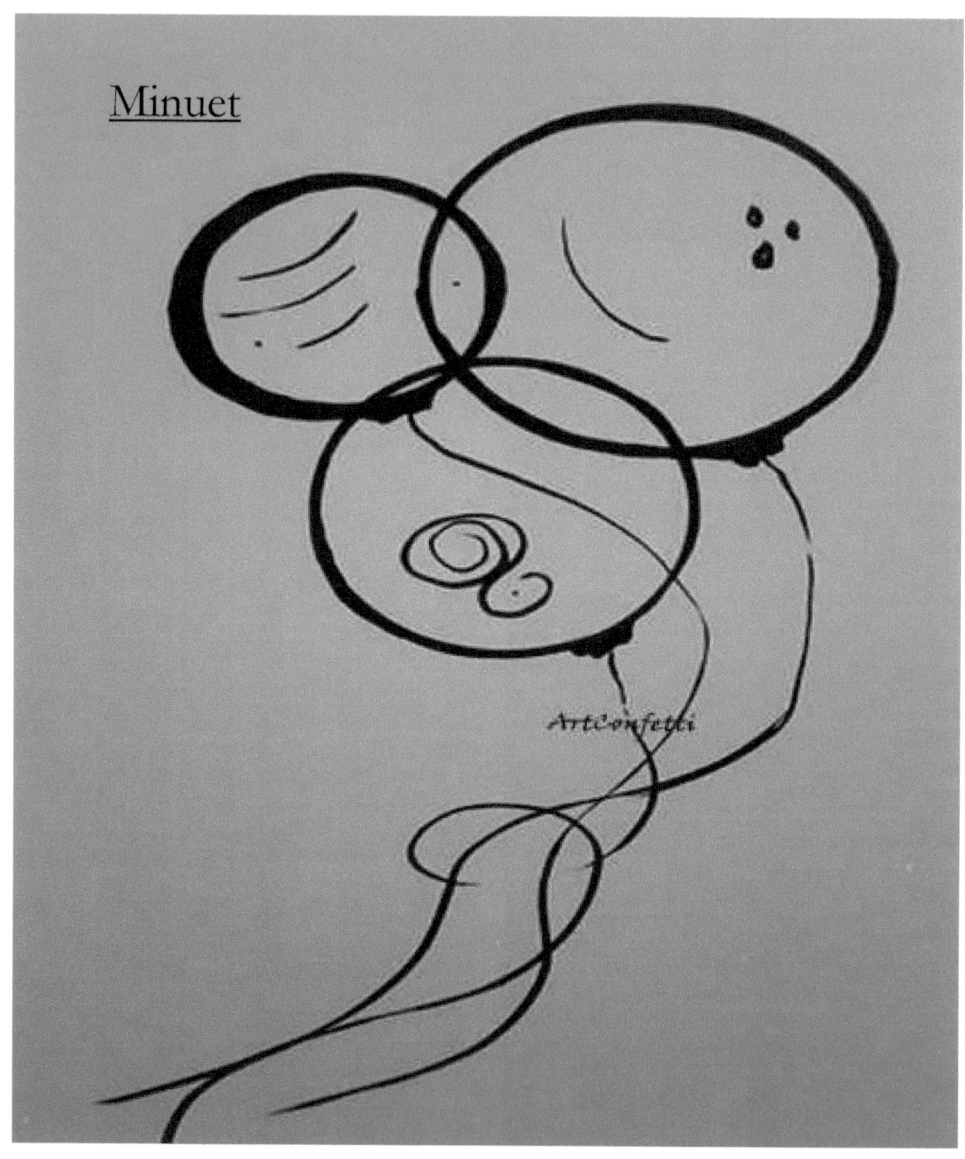

We honor the men who have always tried to treat women well and "do right by them." Those who sometimes have paid a heavy emotional and/or financial price because a predecessor neglected, hurt, mistreated or abandoned a woman and you were penalized just for being male.

We sympathize with women who have tried and tried to hold together a marriage or relationship with a selfish, detached, disinterested or emotionally unavailable man and lost the struggle. We hope to bridge the gap between misbehaving people and the fortunate wonder of souls meeting and genuinely wanting to have and share true love. Relationships are a minuet of strengths, hope and mission, partner with a suitable talent to bind with and tango in life.

ISBN: 9780984647418 – ArtUReady? Ola Gilkey

Copyright © 2017 ArtConfetti All rights reserved.

www.ingramcontent.com/pod-product-compliance
Lightning Source LLC
Chambersburg PA
CBHW042336150426
43195CB00001B/14